Rejection

How to Overcome Deal With Yourself From Rejection

(The Ultimate Guide to Dealing With Rejection and Conquering the Fear of Rejection for Good)

William Yang

Published By **Andrew Zen**

William Yang

*Rejection: How to Overcome Deal With Yourself
From Rejection (The Ultimate Guide to Dealing
With Rejection and Conquering the Fear of
Rejection for Good)*

ISBN 978-0-9952447-1-9

Upon using the information contained in this book, you agree to hold harmless the Author from and against any damages, costs, and expenses, including any legal fees potentially resulting from the application of any of the information provided by this guide. This disclaimer applies to any damages or injury caused by the use and application, whether directly or indirectly, of any advice or information presented, whether for breach of contract, tort, negligence, personal injury, criminal intent, or under any other cause of action.

You agree to accept all risks of using the information presented inside this book. You need to consult a professional medical practitioner in order to ensure you are both able and healthy enough to participate in this program.

No part of this guidebook shall be reproduced in any form without permission in writing from the publisher except in the case of brief quotations embodied in critical articles or reviews.

Legal & Disclaimer

The information contained in this book is not designed to replace or take the place of any form of medicine or professional medical advice. The information in this book has been provided for educational & entertainment purposes only.

The information contained in this book has been compiled from sources deemed reliable, and it is accurate to the best of the Author's knowledge; however, the Author cannot guarantee its accuracy and validity and cannot be held liable for any errors or omissions. Changes are periodically made to this book. You must consult your doctor or get professional medical advice before using any of the suggested remedies, techniques, or information in this book.

Table Of Contents

Chapter 1: The Rsd Wheel Of Rejection Assessment

Now that you have finished the assessment, I want to show you the manner to devise your outcomes on the Wheel of Rejection™ so you can determine when you have RSD.

You ought to have ended up with a total score for each RSD characteristic. An example set of scores is mounted underneath.

In the example table above, the whole rating from every of the characteristics had been introduced collectively, resulting in 280. If you had strongly agreed with each unmarried declaration (i.E. A 5), then the most rating you can advantage is probably 4 hundred. We then calculated which you are 70% likely to have RSD. Here is a summary desk that describes how I could use the resulting percentage to discover the possibility which you have RSD i.E. You suffer from excessive dysphoric rejection.

Whilst knowing the proportion possibility that you be bothered with the aid of RSD based completely totally on the levels from the Wheel of Rejection Assessment™ above, it's also useful to visualise the results to get a enjoy of how many and the manner deeply every function of RSD comes into play for you, whilst rejection takes place.

The rejection wheel can easily be finished by means of way of taking the entire rating of every characteristic and dividing it thru ten and rounding as a end result.

You can download a printable Wheel of Rejection™ image from:

www.Helpwithrsd.Com

Simply use the diagram tested below and located a dot at the right line in every segment. You can then join all the dots and coloration the enclosed vicinity in to get a revel in of the coverage of the tendencies.

Here is an example of a wheel that indicates someone who does struggle with rejection however doesn't fulfill my criteria for RSD.

As you can see they fall into this description based absolutely totally on 59% as they'll be amongst 31-70%: Rejection can be hard on the way to address but you don't pretty tick all of the containers that a person who suffers with RSD might.

Here is an example of someone who doesn't have any indicative characteristics of RSD:

As you could see, they fall into this description based totally totally on 28% as they'll be among 1-30% In this situation we didn't coloration inside the place enclosed with the resource of connecting the dots, truely to expose you that it doesn't affect how you take a look at the ensuing diagram.

Here is an instance of someone who's substantially in all likelihood to be troubled through Rejection Sensitive Dysphoria:

As you can see, they fall into this description primarily based on eighty two% as they will be among 71-ninety% Notice that the enclosed region covers nearly all of the developments that the assessment covers.

So, allow us to recap what we've got were given protected on this financial ruin.

In Chapter Two, I delivered you to the RSD Wheel of Rejection Assessment™ and the way it covers 8 key traits of RSD which I recognized thru non-public experience and statement of others. The assessment consisted of statements which you replied, which indicated the strength to which that function is normal in you.

In this financial ruin, I even have tested you the manner to take the ratings and compute a percent possibility of RSD. I even have moreover tested you techniques to finish the RSD Wheel of Rejection™ so that you can visualise the insurance of RSD throughout each function.

Please maintain in thoughts that there may be no dependable analysis for RSD. This is the principle cause why I developed the RSD Wheel of Rejection Assessment™. It is as a good buy as you to decide whether or no longer or not the consequences are useful to you. If they've got indicated which you are specially in all likelihood suffer from RSD, then you could select to genuinely be given or neglect approximately your cease result.

If you select out to undertake the cease give up end result, it approach you can then go along with the float in advance with the rest of this ebook as I discover some of these traits of RSD in extra detail. You will then be equipped for extra particular strategies for healing thru ingesting later books on this series.

I want that you have located the assessment treasured and insightful. Please depart your comments on our Facebook page by means of the use of way of grabbing the hyperlink from www.Helpwithrsd.Com.

Chapter 2: Emotional Intensity Metaphors

There is an artwork to using metaphors to speak excessive emotions. Let's be honest, it is hard to explain how we sense at the great of days, however for folks that be afflicted by immoderate rejection, the complexity and depth of the feelings professional may be impossible to location into phrases.

In this bankruptcy we're going to find out the emotional depth feature of RSD and introduce you to the thoughts of use metaphors. I actually have written a e-book committed to this method called How to Use Metaphors to Communicate How You Feel. This is the without a doubt one of the books on this series that you can locate on the net website at www.Helpwithrsd.Com

But for now, I need to introduce you to the idea so that you understand how you could leverage metaphors to verbalise (or write down) the way you experience. You can then use this knowledge and knowledge to talk your emotions to your self and others. This will help you grow to be more objective approximately rejection activities which you revel in and be able to recover from them faster.

This manner may even artwork hand-in-hand with the paperback Rejection Event Journal that you may moreover find out on the above net internet site online.

So, what are metaphors?

In a nutshell, metaphors are like secret codes that might convey complex feelings using clean terms and photos. They're wonderful at dressing up emotions, in particular the intense ones, in a manner that makes it lots less tough for you and others to understand. A metaphor might not certainly say that something IS a few aspect else; it paints a colourful photo that touches the imagination.

For example, while you say "I revel in like a deflated balloon," you're not clearly saying you're unhappy or disheartened. You're expressing a deeper feel of loss, disappointment, and exhaustion.

So why are metaphors so powerful? The solution is, they interact our brains in a way that literal language definitely cannot. Metaphors artwork like a well-positioned hook in a catchy song, they draw us in, captivate our interest, and make the enjoy so much greater enjoyable.

Metaphors engage a couple of regions of our brains:

Metaphors do not in reality mild up the language processing areas of our brains; moreover they set off the areas related to sensory and motor skills. That's why on the identical time as someone says, "Life is a roller coaster," you may nearly sense the fun, the united statesand downs, and the adrenaline rush!

Metaphors makes summary requirements concrete:

Emotions are complex. Sometimes they are so precis, it's like looking to capture smoke together with your palms. But metaphors are like a stable field for that smoke. That is a metaphor isn't it! A metaphor can redesign precis emotions into tangible snap shots, making them a good deal much less complex to apprehend and recognize.

Metaphors enhance reminiscence and knowledge:

Our brains are burdened to undergo in mind reminiscences and pictures higher than bloodless records. It's like how you could effects do not forget the plot of your preferred movie but war with recalling a information lecture. Metaphors, with their outstanding imagery and relatability, stick in our reminiscence like peanut butter sticks to the roof of your mouth.

Metaphors Cultivate Empathy:

A metaphor creates a bridge of know-how among human beings. When you describe your feelings the use of metaphors, you invite others into your emotional landscape. It's like giving them a VIP bypass in your private emotional live performance. This can cultivate empathy and make others more attuned to your feelings.

Metaphors are not just quite phrases or linguistic decorations.

So how can we leverage metaphors to present an reason behind the feelings we skilled after rejection event. It's essential that you make an effort after journalling a rejection occasion, as I defined in the Beginners Guide to RSD, to create metaphors across the emotions you skilled.

So, how precisely do you use metaphors to provide an cause at the back of what is going on inner your head and heart?

Identify Your Emotion:

Be the detective at the aspect of your emotions. Are you feeling unhappy? Angry? Frustrated? Confused? Try to label it.

Find Your Metaphor:

Think about what item, state of affairs, or situation can exquisite describe the way you sense. It may be a few factor from a wilting flower to a raging typhoon. Have fun with it!

Describe It:

Dive deeper and describe your metaphor. Are the petals of the wilting flower drooping? Is the storm tearing trees from their roots? This permits paint a extraordinary clearer photograph of your emotions.

Let's take a look at some examples to get your modern juices flowing:

"Feeling rejected looks like a cold wintry weather day, in which the biting wind penetrates your coat and chills you to the bone."

"When criticized, it looks like being a sandcastle washed away through an sudden wave, leaving nothing inside the again of."

"I often sense like an antique, forgotten doll in a toy keep, desperately geared up to be selected and loved."

Remember, those are truely examples. The splendor of metaphors is that they may be specific for your revel in.

To be able to create extra effective metaphors, it's miles going to be useful for me to recap the middle feelings which might be a part of the human revel in.

Core Human Emotions

While there's some debate amongst psychologists about how many middle feelings there sincerely are, most agree on a difficult and fast of number one ones.

1. Joy: It's that bubbly, mild-as-a-feather feeling that consists of happiness, satisfaction, and pride.

2. Sadness: It's the possibility of pleasure. When you feel low, disheartened, or have a

experience of loss, you're experiencing unhappiness.

three. Fear: This is the coronary coronary heart-pounding emotion that jumps out even as you revel in threat or a threat. It may be physical, like a barking canine, or intellectual, just like the worry of failure.

four. Disgust: This is the "eww" feeling you get whilst you stumble upon a few element repulsive, ugly, or offensive. It's now not pretty much rotten meals or gross insects—it may additionally be moral disgust in the direction of unfair practices.

five. Anger: You've possibly met this fiery emotion on the equal time as you have been damage, pissed off, or professional injustice. It's that warm, prickly feeling which can make your blood boil.

6. Surprise: This emotion pops up at the same time as you come upon a few thing unexpected. It's like the gasp you supply while

a chum throws a marvel birthday party for you!

7. Trust: This warm, comforting feeling grows whilst you sense safe and steady with someone or some component. It's what glues relationships and communities collectively.

8. Anticipation: It's the excited buzz you feel earlier than a massive event or alternate. Like the night in advance than your birthday or whilst you're looking in advance to a bundle deal to reach.

Each of these center feelings can be experienced in specific intensities, and that they often mingle with every one of a kind to create more complex emotions that is what takes location within the course of episodes of immoderate rejection.

Also, consider that no emotion is inherently "suitable" or "horrible"—they all are an crucial part of the human enjoy.

I need that this introduction to the usage of metaphors for describing the complexity of

excessive feelings that you revel in all through
rejection, proves treasured to you.

Chapter 3: Rejection Event Frequency Evaluation

In this financial ruin I might be displaying you a manner to affirm the frequency of your rejection sports activities. Throughout this ebook, I will speak over with You and Your however if you are studying this ebook for someone else, then that's good enough too, you can even though comply with along and do the sports activities with them.

So why is it important to understand the frequency of your rejection events so that you can affirm if you'll likely be afflicted by excessive rejection?

The average person does no longer revel in severe rejection that frequently. Perhaps at the identical time as declined for that advertising and advertising and marketing, grew to become down for a date or had their industrial business enterprise concept poo-pooed, then these occasions might be the cause for some feelings of rejection. Those lifestyles sports which could make us enjoy rejected don't display up all that frequently to the commonplace character.

The reality which you are analyzing this ebook approach which you are already privy to rejection touchy dysphoria as a detail, a situation or but you wish to seek advice from it. This is crucial due to the reality, I decided, that the first step to being goal approximately how I turned into feeling, what have become triggering me and the way often it modified into taking place have become keeping apart the me from it.

What do I advise by way of way of this?

Ironically, the best manner to face RSD head on is to now not make it about yourself. Whilst I commit a whole ebook on How To Accept You Have RSD, the first step is sincerely figuring out that the manner you sense is not but inside your manipulate under certain conditions. You must start to cope with RSD as separate to who you're as someone. You aren't RSD or excessive rejection. I need you to take a moment with this idea.

You aren't RSD. You are not intense rejection. There is nothing incorrect with the middle of who you're.

There are styles on your mind that motive severe emotional responses, chemical responses, that you have not however learnt to manipulate and for the instant, that's OK.

You are an great person.

Let's play a small mission. Imagine you're an all righttree. You are a few hundred years vintage with loads of branches and acorns and healthy-searching leaves.

Now ask yourself:

How many humans dislike you?

What's your answer?

It's every going to be, I don't realize or None.

An o.K.Tree can not be rejected but it's miles alive, due to the fact it is truely an all righttree. It is precise as a tree, amongst distinct wood and no unique alrighttree is precisely like it. If the all righttree has a few problem with an infection on its leaves or some decaying bark or a damaged branch, it's far despite the fact that an very welltree. It can recall the decay or the infection as a detail this is hindering its increase, however it isn't a tree of degradation or contamination. It stays a first rate very welltree.

So, place intense rejection, the RSD label outside of your self. You can visual it in a box out of doors of your body as despite the fact that you're looking at it. This is known as disassociation and it's going to serve you well and save you you from beating yourself up on every occasion a rejection occasion takes vicinity.

Imagine there may be water indoors your outdoor area of RSD. You are maintaining the box. The box is out of doors you continuously, manifestly, because it's a box. However, now and again, with out caution, you stumble and the water spills out of the field in your garments. The water spilling out of the world is sort of a rejection event. You mind spills too many chemical compounds into your tool earlier than you have got had been given time to position a place among the manner you instantly apprehend an occasion and logically what is actually taking area.

I desire those analogies will help you separate excessive rejection from who you are in order that even as you log the frequency of your rejection sports activities, you could no longer be tempted to berate yourself or bypass proper into a loop of I'm now not genuine enough.

I pretty suggest grabbing the Rejection Event Journal from the net web page, www.Helpwithrsd.Com as this could help you log the frequency you experience immoderate emotional rejection.

Recap: What is a rejection occasion?

For the purposes of our speak, a rejection occasion are moments on the identical time as you experience intensely rejected. In The Beginners Guide to RSD, I describe some of the feelings you can enjoy at some stage in a rejection event and the inner communicate that would spiral out of control without warning.

A rejection event are the ones moments of immoderate rejection, at the same time as some thing has happened or been said to you or possibly even some thing that you are assuming, that cause you to experience intensely rejected, probably worthless, likely indignant or undesirable. Later in this e-book I may be taking you through a manner to use metaphors to explain the depth of your feelings, however for now you can make certain, that a rejection occasion are those moments on the equal time as you feel intensely rejected.

You understand the best: instantaneous ill for your belly, right now indignant, straight away lack of notion, feeling like you have got got been discarded and so on.

Why is frequency crucial?

In my enjoy, the frequency (i.E. How frequently) you experience rejected, is a real indicator of intense rejection. If you sense rejected every so often, perhaps as soon as every week or more than one instances a month, for my part, I may additionally say that's probably ordinary.

When you begin to take word how of frequently you experience rejected, you may be greatly surprised at how a good deal of your lifestyles you spend managing rejection. Listening to your inner self-talk is like tuning right right right into a radio station this is broadcasting your mind and feelings 24/7. When managing RSD, this station would in all likelihood frequently play the "I've been rejected" song. Your manner is to parent out how often this song is on repeat.

To do this, begin with the useful resource of using dedicating a few moments every day to check in along with your mind. What are they saying? How are they making you experience? Do they make you revel in like you've got were given been rejected or criticized? Paying interest to the ones information is like taking a step again and identifying how frequently the rejection playlist is on a loop.

Understanding this frequency is essential because it enables you gauge the size of the trouble and paves the way for coping techniques. It's like knowing the size of the dragon you are about to slay. Everyone's internal self-speak is specific. There's no proper or wrong, too much or too little. It's about facts your patterns and rhythm. Awareness is the primary, and regularly, the most big step toward change.

So, are you equipped to track into your radio station?

I prepare some examples of internal dialogues that might occur while you experience rejected. It's essential to don't forget, despite the fact that, anyone's inner voice is particular, and those are honestly feasible examples:

Why do I typically mess subjects up? No surprise they do not need me spherical.

I should have stated a few component incorrect again. They appeared so aggravated with me.

I knew it. I'm in truth no longer accurate sufficient. They've placed a person higher.

They did now not encompass me due to the truth they in all likelihood do not like me.

I am a burden to them. That's why they avoid spending time with me.

I can not do something right. They must think I'm a failure.

They didn't respond to my message. They need to be dissatisfied with me.

Why do I even attempt? I sincerely turn out to be getting rejected.

They laughed after I tripped. They want to assume I'm a shaggy dog story.

I failed to get invited to the party. They in all likelihood do now not need me there.

When you capture your self having those forms of self-talk, it's far important to mission them with compassion and information. Rejection frequently says more about the scenario or the other person than approximately you.

If you're experiencing rejection more than one times constant with day, then this is disproportionate and when you have already taken the RSD Wheel of Rejection Assessment™ you could recognise the probability of whether or not or not you already go through with RSD.

Before we waft on, a query to do not forget is:

Should I tell the alternative individual every time I enjoy rejected?

Sharing your feelings of rejection, whether or no longer or no longer the use of metaphors or not, may be a double-edged sword. On the upside, expressing your feelings to someone you acquire as right with can offer comfort and emotions of being understood. It's like freeing a pressure valve, that would prevent emotions from constructing as much as an explosive degree. You benefit a very specific attitude at the rejection occasion that appears so excessive to you. Sometimes, what seems like a harsh rejection to you may appear as a simple false impression to an interloper.

However, at the turn side, constantly sharing your emotions of rejection may additionally moreover have a few drawbacks. It may additionally additionally inadvertently create a self-enjoyable prophecy, in that you're normally seeking out rejection and finding it even though it is not there. This regular hobby on lousy emotions may be emotionally arduous for each you and the man or woman you are confiding in. Plus, it could inadvertently positioned a stress in your dating, mainly if the possibility man or woman starts offevolved offevolved feeling beaten or uncertain of the manner to help.

I might also want to take into account sharing your emotions the use of metaphors defined inside the previous bankruptcy, but moreover make investments time in developing self-soothing techniques and re-framing terrible self-talk. If you feel you have got a person near you who you could accept as true with and is familiar with that you frequently feel rejected, you could test sharing your feelings with them the use of the metaphors you have got created.

Chapter 4: Physical Response Mapping

One of the things that constantly amazed me the maximum throughout moments of intense rejection emerge as the bodily responses within the body to the notion of the scenario. These responses have been regularly uncontrollable, however what need to be blamed for them. I would shake uncontrollably, have a thumping heart and my lips would preserve on with my tooth.

PMy cause for you on this financial disaster is that will help you chart the responses introduced about within you by means of the acute feelings skilled inside the path of rejection.

Why is it critical to do this and the manner does it assist in records if you do in reality be troubled through RSD?

Assuming you have got had been given finished the RSD Wheel of Rejection Assessment™ you want to have a excellent idea through now whether or now not or not you suffer from intense rejection. One of the traits of RSD that the evaluation focused on have become our reactions to rejection perceived or actual. These reactions embody our physical responses.

So, identifying when you have a bodily response to severe rejection goes that will help you make bigger a deeper experience of whether or not you be stricken by manner of RSD.

The key right proper here is to understand which you are growing an interest of bodily responses which you usually have. Your physical responses may well be specific to mine, but information what yours are will help you apprehend whilst you are experiencing rejection.

For instance:

"Why am I shaking uncontrollably due to the reality he/she said...?"

Your physical responses can then also become a cue for you to say to your self:

"hi there, a few issue immoderate goes on proper right here proper now, so possibly I can in fact step decrease lower again a chunk as I am maximum in all likelihood going into excessive rejection"

Understanding the Body-Emotion Connection

So, I want to find out the hyperlink between our emotions and our our our bodies, with You. Emotions, particularly the ones associated with extreme rejection, can seem physical. Our our our bodies are giving us signs of our emotional u . S . A ..

Have there been moments of worry or tension even as your coronary coronary coronary heart pounded quicker? Or instances whilst your hands have emerge as damp? These bodily reactions are signs, indicating the presence of sturdy feelings. In this speak amongst frame and feelings, your frame communicates its distress in a profound, however silent, way.

The dating among body and feelings isn't one-directional. Your feelings can motive physical modifications, at the same time as your bodily nation can also effect your emotions. For instance, shallow, quick respiratory can growth feelings of anxiety, on the identical time as deeper, slower breaths have to have a calming effect.

Understanding this connection is vital for you at the same time as navigating the intense feelings associated with RSD. By spotting the physical signs that accompany those emotions, you gain perception into your emotional country. This cognizance won't make the ache of rejection disappear, however it'll assist you to manage your emotions greater correctly.

As you emerge as extra in-song to your frame's reactions, you build a deeper facts of your self. This information lays the foundation for developing strategies to cope with the emotional turbulence due to excessive rejection. Recognizing and acknowledging your frame's responses are critical steps on this manner.

The connection amongst your feelings and your frame is a effective one, with every element responding to the opposite. Understanding this connection and recognizing your specific bodily responses to feelings suggests that you are taking private duty in your emotions and reviews of rejection.

Basic Physiology of Emotional Response

Considering the physiological element of emotional responses can provide us with a better expertise of what is taking area to us during a rejection event.

To higher understand the body's responses, it's nicely worth information the feature of the demanding gadget. It has sizeable additives that come into play: the sympathetic and parasympathetic structures. The sympathetic system turns on the 'combat or flight' response at the same time as dealing with traumatic conditions. This activation can bring about signs and symptoms which consist of speedy respiratory, improved coronary heart fee, and heightened alertness.

On the opportunity hand, the parasympathetic system is liable for the 'relaxation and digest' kingdom. It calms the body down after a annoying event, slowing the heart price and returning the body to a country of equilibrium. It's like a integrated gadget for restoring balance after emotional upheaval.

So, while confronted with excessive feelings collectively with rejection, the sympathetic system may probable kick into excessive tools, critical to a cascade of physical symptoms and signs. Paying hobby to those symptoms and symptoms can tell you about the depth of your emotional response.

Additionally, the body uses numerous hormones, like cortisol and adrenaline, to manage disturbing situations. These hormones can result in physical adjustments which includes extended heart fee, extended blood stress, and heightened recognition. By spotting the ones changes, you could bring together a higher know-how of your emotional nation.

Using the Rejection Event Journal (visit www.Helpwithrsd.Com) will help you in monitoring the bodily responses and emotional states of your rejection activities.

Lastly, anyone's physiological reaction is specific, and it's miles important to phrase that exquisite emotions can evoke extremely good responses. For instance, fear would probable purpose a cold sweat, whilst anger can also result in flushed pores and skin.

So, through the usage of using records these physiological responses and their dating with our feelings, you may greater effortlessly recognize your frame's indicators. This information will help you expand greater powerful techniques to control extreme emotions that arise in RSD.

Mapping Core Emotions to Physical Responses

So, as you likely recognize through now, I like to provide easy strategies for conceptualising and managing complex matters. I need to show you the manner to map your core feelings to the real physical experience you have were given, sooner or later of a rejection event.

But first, information the relationship between our emotions and bodily responses is probably lots less tough by looking at specific examples. Let's check the center human emotions we referred to in advance, such as worry, unhappiness, and anger, all of which can be stirred with the resource of rejection, and notice how they are able to occur bodily.

Fear, regularly the primary reaction to rejection, can trigger a variety of physical responses. These may additionally include a racing coronary coronary heart, shortness of breath, or a experience of tightness within the chest. Your frame is getting equipped for a 'combat or flight' response.

Sadness, every one of a kind not unusual emotion tied to rejection, need to bring about adjustments like a decrease in electricity, a experience of heaviness, or maybe disruptions in sleep patterns. It's the body's way of encouraging us to slow down and manner our feelings.

Then there's anger, which may also furthermore cease cease end result from repeated memories of rejection. Physically, you may feel warmth rushing to your face, your coronary coronary coronary heart pounding, or your fingers clenching. These are symptoms and signs and signs your body is gearing as a whole lot as confront the difficulty.

Building a more complete map of feelings includes thinking about a broader range of emotional responses. Along with fear, disappointment, and anger, there are various other middle feelings like marvel, disgust, and delight, which, despite the fact that less frequently, additionally may be linked with reports of rejection.

Surprise, as an instance, can get up whilst rejection is surprising. This emotion may moreover moreover cause a shocking intake of breath, widened eyes, or possibly a puff. Your frame is signalling the need to absorb new data fast.

Disgust is a few other emotion that may stand up in high quality rejection situations. You could in all likelihood experience your nostril wrinkling, a sour taste in your mouth, or a churn in your stomach. These reactions can be your frame's way of expressing distaste or repulsion.

Joy, alternatively, may also seem out of region in a talk approximately rejection. However, times wherein expected rejection does no longer stand up can in reality elicit pleasure. Physically, this can appear as snug muscle groups, a lightness within the chest, or an involuntary smile.

As daft as it sounds, I have been recognised to chortle as an involuntary reaction to rejection. How unusual is that!

Additionally, emotions together with guilt, disgrace, or consolation also can take a look at research of rejection. Each of these feelings, too, have precise physical responses which might be absolutely really well worth noting and knowledge.

By broadening the scope of emotions and their associated physical responses, we're capable of beautify our records of our frame's language. This multiplied map not satisfactory offers a useful view of our emotional panorama however also strengthens our potential to cope with the extreme emotions professional at some stage in a rejection occasion:

So, each emotion has a tendency to have related physical responses. Recognizing what yours are, might be very treasured, providing insights into your emotional state. By mapping those responses, you may build a higher data of your body's verbal exchange style, equipping you to govern your emotions more effectively.

So, here's a certainly clean way to assemble that map. Complete the table beneath with the physical responses you frequently revel in throughout immoderate rejection after which write down the corresponding emotion. It doesn't keep in mind if its an professional middle emotion, sincerely write down the phrase meaning the most to you. For example. You may additionally additionally use the terms scared as hell in preference to worry.

Your Response Strategy

After recognizing your specific physiological signs, the following step is growing a custom designed reaction approach. This involves devising techniques to address the physical responses arising from rejection-induced feelings. By understanding your body's cues, you may higher control the ones feelings and their bodily manifestations.

Your response method will rely in big element on the bodily signs and symptoms you revel in. If feelings of rejection result in a racing coronary heart or fast breathing, for instance, deep respiration sporting activities or meditation may be powerful equipment to gradual your coronary heart price and calm your respiratory.

Similarly, if anxiety headaches or muscle tightness are your body's response to rejection, physical hobby which incorporates stretching or yoga is probably beneficial. These sports no longer best alleviate the bodily ache however also can help modify emotional misery.

For disenchanted stomach or lack of urge for food, finding calming sports or rest techniques may be a useful technique. This would possibly include paying attention to soothing tune, on foot in nature, or sporting out a hobby that brings you delight.

You also can comprise strategies which includes cognitive-behavioral strategies or mindfulness into your reaction plan. These processes assist you to cope with the underlying emotions tied in your physical signs, promoting a extra healthy emotional kingdom.

Your custom designed reaction method is a dynamic plan that can be changed as needed. As you broaden and your information of your frame-emotion connection evolves, your strategies may additionally moreover need to adjust too. This adaptability is a strength, allowing you to commonly refine your approach primarily based to your cutting-edge-day desires.

By proactively addressing your bodily signs and symptoms, you're not handiest coping with the instantaneous soreness however additionally acknowledging and validating your emotional enjoy. This way fosters a nurturing relationship with yourself, allowing you to address immoderate feelings with extended resilience and self-compassion.

I preference which you have decided this exploration of the manner the intense feelings you revel in with RSD can be mapped to physical responses and then how you could leverage the bodily cues to boom similarly clarity as to whether or not or now not you undergo with RSD.

Chapter 5: Perceived Or Real

What of some thing is genuinely actual? We have a observe the area through our eyes, interacting with our senses. For neuro-everyday humans, achieving balance between what's without a doubt taking place round them and the manner they perceive the ones occasions, is typically carefully related. For someone experiencing the intense emotions of rejection, the perception of what they're experiencing is regularly precise to what's going on in front of them.

So, at some point of this ebook we have been supporting you discover in case you suffer from RSD through exploring the developments of it. Many of those developments are pushed through our belief of rejection.

For example, if recognize that you are being rejected it can cause self-loathing, avoidance strategies and looping. It's crucial therefore that we make the effort to recall how your belief is probably providing strong symptoms that you be by means of RSD, in addition to developing attention about belief in place of fact.

I am no longer saying that everybody who studies excessive rejection is out of contact with reality, as an opportunity we are exploring how our notion of rejection is out of sync with any real rejection.

Imagine your accomplice said:

"I don't like that get dressed on you".

For a person with RSD, this could cause an excessive rejection occasion, however in truth, it's just a comment which even as said to a person who doesn't be stricken by way of intense rejection, they might probably reply with.

"Well, I like it" or "Which get dressed do you make a decision upon".

It's vital that we attempt to differentiate some of the event of rejection itself and our perception of that occasion. These   aren't generally identical. Our mind is a complex entity and its interpretation of studies can extensively shape our fact. This is especially apparent at the same time as handling emotionally immoderate studies collectively with rejection. Let's explore how severe emotions of rejection may additionally distort our notion of truth and the manner we would separate the perceived from the real. By doing this, you would likely find out new insights approximately your personal tales and the manner your perception colours them.

What is Perception?

Perception, in reality positioned, is our interpretation of the sector round us. It's how we make enjoy of our tales, guided by way of the usage of the usage of our senses, emotions, thoughts, beyond studies, or even our cultural and social contexts. The way of belief is complicated, concerning severa cognitive and neurological strategies that art work together to form our knowledge and interpretation of sports activities.

In the context of rejection, our notion performs a good sized function. It impacts now not absolutely how we recognize the occasion of rejection, however moreover how we reply to it. For example, endure in mind two people who didn't get a task they performed for. One might apprehend this as a personal failure and sense intensely rejected. In assessment, the alternative may also see it as a minor setback and an opportunity for boom.

Perception, in this revel in, drastically affects our emotional reaction. This is because of the reality our brain has a bent to create narratives spherical our evaluations, and people narratives, fuelled via our feelings, shape our perception. When dealing with an emotionally excessive experience like rejection, those narratives may be specially powerful, frequently blurring the traces among what is perceived and what is actual.

How does rejection impact our perceptions?

When we experience rejection, our thoughts often goes right right into a defensive mode, looking to make enjoy of this painful experience. This gadget can increase our horrible emotions and create a distorted notion of the event and of ourselves.

This distortion might also moreover lead us to perceive rejection in which it is able to no longer exist, or interpret neutral situations as rejecting. For instance, a pal no longer responding right now to a textual content message is probably perceived as rejection. Here, the actual occasion — a pal now not responding immediately — is seen via a lens tinted with the fear and anticipation of rejection. This outcomes in a perceived rejection that might not align with truth.

Intense feelings of rejection may moreover lead us to overgeneralize, taking a selected event of rejection and making use of it broadly. For instance, getting rejected in a task interview also can purpose thoughts like,

"I'm typically a failure" or "No one will ever hire me". These perceptions paint a fact that is broader and greater absolute than the actual event warrants.

Examples of Perceived vs. Real Rejection

To illustrate the distinction between perceived and real rejection, allow's recall a few common situations. Imagine you're at a occasion, and a pal seems to spend greater time speakme to others than with you. The fact of the scenario might be that the friend is truely catching up with people they have no longer visible in some time. However, beneath the impact of excessive rejection emotions, you will likely understand this as them keeping off you or who determine on the agency of others.

Or, recollect a state of affairs in which your concept isn't decided on in a collection meeting at artwork. The reality can be that there had been severa nicely thoughts, and the satisfactory that suit the assignment excellent grow to be selected. However, if your thoughts is clouded by way of manner of rejection, you might understand this as a personal slight, interpreting it as your crew not valuing your contributions.

By statistics the distinction among the ones perceived and actual situations of rejection, you begin to understand the effect of your perceptions and the narratives they devise.

Self-Reflection and Awareness

Building self-awareness is prime to distinguishing between perceived and actual rejection. A aware method can be quite useful proper right here. When an event triggers emotions of rejection, in area of at once reacting, pause and ask your self, "Is this rejection actual, or is it my notion? What evidence do I truely have?"

Keeping a mag which include with the aid of using the usage of the Rejection Event Journal moreover can be beneficial. When you enjoy rejected, write about the occasion, your emotions, and why you trust you've got been rejected. Later, at the equal time as your emotions have settled, revisit the access and objectively have a look at if the rejection modified into real or perceived.

Over time, these practices will allow you to grow to be more aware about your notion styles, perceptions, and emotional responses, offering valuable insights into your non-public reviews of rejection.

Discerning Perception from Reality

Once you've constructed a strong basis of self-popularity, you may begin to actively figure perception from truth. One useful method is truth-checking. When you revel in emotions of rejection, test the facts. What sincerely came about? Try to cut up the data from your feelings and assumptions.

Another technique is searching for out of doors perspectives. Discussing your evaluations with depended on buddies or a highbrow health expert can provide opportunity viewpoints and assist you recognize the scenario more objectively.

Cognitive restructuring techniques, regularly utilized in cognitive-behavioural therapy, additionally may be effective. This includes identifying and difficult irrational or negative thoughts and beliefs, and converting them with greater rational, balanced perspectives.

Coping with Perceived Rejection

Dealing with perceived rejection includes every managing the intense emotions delivered about and changing the perception itself. Emotional law strategies, along with deep respiratory, mindfulness, and physical hobby, can help control emotional misery.

To alter the notion, cognitive strategies may be effective. This includes reframing terrible thoughts, that specialize in first-rate components, and training self-compassion. Remember, it's good enough to revel in hurt with the aid of manner of manner of perceived rejection. It doesn't make your emotions lots less valid. What topics is the way you deal with those feelings and paintings on shifting your perception to align more with fact.

Rejection, whether or now not perceived or actual, can be a hard experience. But with attention, understanding, and powerful strategies, you can navigate thru it with resilience, developing a extra healthy dating with your self and your perceptions.

Chapter 6: Avoidance Strategies

When faced with stories that would reason rejection, it is pretty natural for us to attempt to shield ourselves. One way we frequently do this is through the usage of avoidance techniques

So, what are avoidance techniques within the context of RSD?

The are behaviours or techniques we use to bypass situations that we assume may bring about emotional distress or pain, along aspect excessive rejection. This is our mind's manner of safeguarding our emotional nicely-being. However, the ones strategies need to restrict your opportunities, restrict your relationships, and stall your personal boom, specifically if carefully depend upon them.

By understanding what those strategies are and why we use them, we can discover ways to control them efficiently and growth extra healthful strategies of coping with ability rejection.

Avoidance and Fear of Rejection

Avoidance techniques and worry of rejection are cautiously related. The idea of being rejected may be specially daunting, specially for those people who're pretty sensitive to rejection. This fear can cause a protecting response, pushing us to keep away from situations wherein we'd revel in rejection.

For instance, you'll probable decline invitations to social sports due to the truth you are concerned you may now not in form in, or you will possibly avoid asking for help because of the truth you are involved about being visible as incompetent. In each situations, the underlying fear of rejection is using the avoidance behaviour.

Do you recognize any of these styles in yourself?

Remember, that avoidance is one of the characteristics that we evaluated on the identical time as you took the RSD Wheel of Rejection Assessment™. This financial break will add in addition readability as to whether or not or now not or no longer you be anxious via RSD primarily based totally mostly on the outcomes of your evaluation, collectively with presenting you with a deeper know-how about avoidance techniques that could resonate with how you're behaving.

This relationship amongst avoidance and fear of rejection isn't quite lots on foot far from unsightly reviews. It's additionally approximately striving for a sense of protection and recognition. When we use avoidance strategies, we are looking to create a fact wherein we are a good deal much less probable to face rejection a place wherein we enjoy normal and customary.

Common Examples of Avoidance Strategies

Avoidance strategies can take many bureaucracy, and that they'll be pretty subtle, making them difficult to discover. Here are some examples to offer you an idea:

Procrastination: This includes disposing of duties that could possibly purpose rejection or complaint. For example, you may postpone submitting a venture at paintings due to the truth you're demanding about receiving negative comments.

Withdrawal from social conditions: If you're worried approximately being rejected in social settings, you could restriction your social interactions. You might in all likelihood decline invites, avoid starting conversations, or remain quiet in institution discussions.

Overcompensating in relationships: You can also try to be overly accommodating or agreeable in relationships to avoid conflicts that might purpose rejection. You can also locate yourself agreeing with others even while you don't simply percentage their reviews, or going from your manner to please them.

Not voicing your dreams: Fear of rejection could in all likelihood keep you lower lower lower back from expressing your want and goals. You would probable fear that others might reject you in case you seem disturbing or needy.

Avoiding new opportunities: You might hesitate to try new subjects, like utilizing for a marketing or beginning a new interest, due to worry of failure and next rejection.

Recognizing the ones behaviours in your self is the first step closer to handling your avoidance techniques.

The Psychology Behind Avoidance

To efficaciously address our avoidance techniques, it is useful to apprehend the highbrow methods underlying them. Avoidance behaviour is basically pushed thru a intellectual concept called horrible reinforcement. Negative reinforcement takes region even as the elimination of an unpleasant stimulus (like worry or anxiety) reinforces a particular behaviour (like avoidance). So, at the same time as we avoid situations that might motive rejection, we enjoy a quick remedy from fear and anxiety. This remedy strengthens the avoidance behaviour, making us much more likely to duplicate it inside the future.

Another highbrow problem at play is the self-attractive prophecy, in which our ideals and expectations unconsciously have an effect on our movements, foremost to effects that verify those beliefs. For instance, if we anticipate to be rejected, we might unconsciously behave in strategies that result in rejection, thereby confirming our preliminary perception.

Understanding these mental standards allows us to see that while our avoidance techniques might likely provide short-term consolation, they may make stronger our fears and insecurities within the long term. But undergo in mind, we are not powerless in the direction of those patterns. By recognizing and know-how them, we equip ourselves with the tools to interrupt loose from them.

Identifying Your Avoidance Strategies

Now which you have a draw close on what avoidance strategies are and why you is probably using them, it is time to start figuring out your private techniques. This step is essential because it lets in you to understand while and why you operate avoidance, assisting you wreck the cycle.

A first step in this manner may be self-pondered photograph. Take some quiet moments for yourself and reflect onconsideration on times even as you have got felt excessive worry of rejection. What did you do in response to the ones emotions? Did you withdraw, procrastinate, or overcompensate?

Keeping a magazine additionally can be useful. Every day, make a be aware of any situations in that you felt the urge to use an avoidance technique. Write down the scenario, the manner you felt, and what you possibly did in response. Over time, you may start to phrase styles for your behaviour that you hadn't seen in advance than.

Remember, this method is not approximately judging yourself; it's far approximately knowledge your self better. So, method it with interest and kindness.

Impact of Avoidance Strategies

As you've got probable positioned thru now, at the identical time as avoidance strategies could probably assist you keep away from emotions of rejection within the brief time period, they frequently aren't beneficial in the long run. Yes, they may be capable of provide a brief revel in of relief from anxiety or worry, however they do not help you address or conquer those emotions.

Over time, reliance on avoidance strategies can result in a cycle in that you feel developing fear and tension, predominant you to keep away from more, which in turn reinforces your fears. This cycle can restriction your possibilities for personal growth, damage your relationships, and negatively effect your shallowness and self-self perception.

Moreover, constantly preserving off capability rejection can imply you omit out on reviews and possibilities that would cause private increase, improved talents, or deeper connections with others.

Alternatives to Avoidance

While it is straightforward that avoidance strategies aren't the tremendous response to fear of rejection, there are greater healthy alternatives. These techniques focus on confronting the priority of rejection straight away, growing resilience, and boosting self-esteem.

One such technique is mindfulness, which includes staying gift in the 2nd and accepting your mind and emotions without judgment. When confronted with capacity rejection, in desire to resorting to avoidance, you could have a observe and well known your emotions of fear and tension. This attention can lessen the strength those emotions have over you and assist you reply in a greater in form manner.

Another method is cognitive reframing, which entails converting the way you interpret and bear in mind a scenario. For example, in vicinity of viewing a potential rejection as a threat, you may view it as an possibility for analyzing and boom.

If you commit to constructing your vanity and feature compassion for your self, you can become more resilient to ability rejection. This may want to likely include acknowledging your strengths, working towards self-care, and reminding your self that everybody research rejection and it does no longer reflect your certainly well worth or price.

Making a Personalized Plan to Overcome Avoidance

Now which you recognize your avoidance techniques and characteristic some alternatives in thoughts, it is time to position this data into motion. You can try this by the use of developing a custom designed plan to conquer your avoidance behaviour.

Start via the use of identifying the conditions in which you generally will be predisposed to apply avoidance strategies. Then, pick out one or alternatives that you think can be simply right for you inside the ones situations. Make a plan for the way you may located into effect the ones options the subsequent time you're confronted with capability rejection.

Changing long-reputation behaviour styles takes time and staying power. You may not get it right on every occasion, and this is ok. What's important is that you're growing a conscious attempt to break the cycle of avoidance and fear.

I choice that this bankruptcy has furnished you with a similarly opportunity to apprehend if you be bothered via RSD through looking more deeply at one in each of its developments – avoidance.

Chapter 7: Personal Impact Analysis

As we method the forestall of this diploma of your journey in figuring out if you have RSD, it felt right that will help you apprehend how severe rejection impacts you at a private stage. The reason here isn't to place blame or stay on negatives. Instead, it's far approximately growing self-popularity, developing empathy for your self, and gaining perception into how you can shape a extra healthful destiny.

In this financial ruin, I check how the worry of rejection is probably influencing your lifestyles from yourself-belief and relationships in your choice-making and health. As you have a look at, undergo in our mind that everybody's experience is precise, and it is okay if no longer the whole thing resonates with you.

Rejection and Self-Perception

We noted belief instead of reality in a previous financial disaster. One of the brilliant ways rejection can effect you is through yourself-perception. It can chip away at your vanity, making you doubt your clearly really worth and abilties. If you often sense rejected, you would probably begin believing that there can be a few issue essentially wrong with you, most essential to feelings of loss of self belief and inadequacy.

These styles of ideals can affect your attitude, inflicting you to interpret impartial or ambiguous occasions as rejection. For instance, if a chum does not without delay respond in your message, you can anticipate they will be ignoring you due to the fact they may be displeased with you, even as they might simply be busy.

This altered self-belief can inadvertently cause more critiques of rejection. If you count on to be rejected, you may behave in ways that inspire that very last effects, collectively with retreating from others or performing defensively.

Effects on Relationships

Fear of rejection can extensively have an impact in your relationships. You can also find your self averting closeness or self-discipline due to the worry that you will be rejected as quickly as others get to understand you higher. You ought to probable struggle to explicit your feelings and goals, worrying that doing so may additionally cause conflict and capability rejection.

These behaviours can create distance and misconception on your relationships, preventing you from forming deep, pleasurable connections. They also can cause you to miss out on potential relationships because of the truth you pre-emptively reject others to keep away from being rejected yourslf.

In the context of gift relationships, steady worry about rejection might purpose you to misinterpret your circle of relatives' moves, seeing rejection in which there may be none. This can purpose vain battle and stress the relationship.

Impact on Decision Making

Living with a continual fear of rejection may additionally have a big affect on your choice-making manner. You may discover your self continuously choosing the 'secure' preference to keep away from potential rejection or criticism. For example, you may decline a vending due to the fact you're concerned about the prolonged visibility and potential for rejection, or you will possibly avoid expressing your opinion in company settings out of fear of being disagreed with.

This hazard-avoidant behaviour can restriction your possibilities for increase and fulfilment. You should probable bypass over out on exciting possibilities because of your fear, and this can reason emotions of regret and frustration. It also can contribute to feelings of being 'stuck', as you may hesitate to make adjustments or take steps in advance even while you're disappointed collectively collectively together with your cutting-edge-day state of affairs.

Physical Health Consequences

Chronic stress related to fear of rejection can take area physical, main to numerous health problems. You would probable discover it tough to sleep, revel in common headaches, or extend digestive problems. Over time, those issues can effect your easy fitness, contributing to situations like coronary heart disease and a weakened immune device.

Mental Health Consequences

Experiencing excessive rejection can considerably impact your highbrow health. Anxiety is a common final results, wherein you can find out yourself in a regular country of fear, continuously searching forward to the next rejection to hit. This country of hyper-vigilance can drain you emotionally, leaving you feeling fatigued and even purpose burnout.

Depression is any other viable outcome of repeated tales of immoderate rejection. If you regularly experience rejected, you may start believing that you're unlovable or nugatory, main to emotions of hopelessness and unhappiness. You may become bored in sports activities you used to enjoy or find out it difficult to inspire yourself to get through the day.

Furthermore, intense worry of rejection can result in social anxiety disease, in which you enjoy overwhelming anxiety and immoderate self-recognition in everyday social conditions. You can also moreover dread social events, worry excessively about them ahead, or avoid them absolutely to prevent capability rejection.

Again, these are possibilities, now not certainties. Experiencing rejection does now not imply you can constantly face the ones highbrow fitness worrying conditions. However, being privy to these risks let you take steps in the direction of prevention and early intervention.

Quality of Life and Life Satisfaction

Intense fear of rejection will have an effect in your regular fine of existence and existence satisfaction. When you constantly fear about rejection, it's difficult to enjoy your studies absolutely. You is probably physical present however mentally preoccupied with fears and insecurities.

The worry of rejection also can save you you from pursuing your passions, desires, or dreams. You may keep your self decrease decrease back from possibilities due to the capability for rejection. This self-limiting behaviour can depart you feeling unfulfilled and discontented together with your existence.

Your relationships, career, and pastimes elements that appreciably make contributions to life pleasure can all be hampered by using way of a continual fear of rejection. By spotting and addressing this fear, you can improve your satisfactory of lifestyles and beautify your normal properly-being.

Sex and Intimacy

When rejection seeps proper proper right into a relationship, it is able to have an effect at the sexual dynamics among companions. If you have immoderate rejection sensitivity, those impacts can be even extra big. The worry and anticipation of rejection can stir up a soup of emotions, fundamental to a cascade of reactions that would have an impact on the intimacy to your dating.

Firstly, the anticipation of rejection can result in anxiety, which is often a roadblock to sexual choice. It can create a immoderate-stress surroundings wherein it will become difficult to enjoy cushty and cushty enough for sexual hobby. You can also discover yourself preoccupied with mind of capacity rejection, which can detract out of your capability to be present and engaged in the second.

This worry need to make it difficult to talk overtly approximately sexual dreams and barriers. Effective verbal exchange is a critical detail of a satisfying sexual courting, and whilst clouded via the priority of rejection, it could result in dissatisfaction and false impression. You could probable suppress your very personal goals, fearing that expressing them would possibly bring about rejection through manner of your companion.

Rejection in a sexual context can also cause decreased vanity and frame photograph issues. Sexuality is carefully related with vulnerability and popularity. Experiencing rejection, whether perceived or actual, would in all likelihood make you query your beauty or desirability, that can further have an effect for your sexual self assure and entertainment.

Try to recognize the ones affects and recognize that it is perfectly k to attempting to find help. Conversations collectively along with your accomplice, self-love and reputation practices, or maybe professional assist from a therapist can assist in navigating thru the ones demanding situations. Intimacy is not pretty much the act itself, however moreover about the comfort, acquire as real with, and records you percent together along with your associate.

As we come to the give up of this financial ruin, it is important to endure in thoughts that experiencing severe rejection isn't a private failing or weak spot. It's part of your adventure, and each step you are taking towards know-how and recuperation is a testomony on your power and resilience.

Owning your tale consists of acknowledging your tales, knowledge their impacts, and taking steps to navigate via your fears. It's not about wiping out the concern of rejection in fact — this is an unrealistic expectation, thinking about that everyone, to a few diploma, fears rejection. Instead, it's about growing the capability to control whilst the fear arises.

The method may want to probably seem hard, and that's k. You're now not by myself on this journey. There are assets and helps available that will help you through it, collectively with therapists, help agencies, and self-assist books. Remember, it is not most effective about the holiday spot but additionally about the adventure. Each step you're taking is a step in the path of a more empowered, resilient, and self-compassionate you.

Chapter 8: How To Recognize Rejection

How has your enjoy been asking a person out or confessing on your weigh down? How did they react? Often people will react for your love interest in an uncertain way. . You want to first decide whether or not or not or no longer you've got been refused earlier than figuring out the manner to maintain.

1. Try to Plan an Outing With Them.

Make plans to satisfy up with them. Pay interest to how people react. Acting subdued or irritable might also moreover moreover imply he is trying to civilly decline your invitation.

If you're requested out, be super. Don't assume you have already been grew to become down. You must say "Can we meet soonest?

So make your invitation as easy as possible.

Try coming near the person. It's a high-quality indicator if they will be interested by talking to you. If you have a examine this character avoiding you, they will be attempting to tell you that they do now not along with you. Choose a unique hobby and hour. It's easy to say "sure" on every occasion you request someone to "spend a while with you." That's due to the truth they're no longer in all likelihood to must bring it out. Ask the individual to meet you at a selected time or area.

Give an opinion you apprehend they'll love. If they'll be enthusiastic about sports sports, you can invite them to a recreation. Suggest seeing a film collectively in case you're each thrilled about it. They're probably to reject you if they may be lacking some element that that they had despite the fact that love to do.

It can be hard to trade the time or hobby. If you've already been rejected. You might not be capable of determine the motive for the rejection till you find out some other answer.

Keep it sincere. You ought to say "Are you to be had to examine a film this weekend? However, I might be going to the beachside on Saturday. Would that pique your interest?"

It's an excellent indicator in case your invitation is conventional this time. The truth that they're busy also can mean that they'll take delivery of you irrespective of their busy time desk.

If they decline to conform with a time and date or forget about your second recommendation, they is probably seeking to refuse you.

Encourage them to the touch you if they may be inquisitive about spending time with you. . There's no component in persevering with with a person who probable isn't interested. Let them recognise they may come over in the event that they need to visit you. This places the ball again of their courtroom docket docket, allowing you to select up your lifestyles all yet again.

Always live excessive great no matter how angry or discouraged you're. Avoid appearing sour or green with envy. At the give up of the day, you are every unique souls with sizable talents and tastes.

You should say, "You appear busy right now. If you like to speak with me, touch me on my cellular cellphone." You want to be prepared for the opportunity that they may now not touch you, notwithstanding the reality that they may be in possession of the ball.

2. Maintain Contact With Them.

Check to look inside the occasion that they ever start touch. Are you the handiest that constantly initiates a textual content verbal exchange or says hi there at the same time as you spot each exclusive? Do you find it hard to have a verbal exchange or deliver an electronic mail? If you are constantly the number one to start or keep a communication, they may be looking for to distance themselves from you. Make a telephone call to them. Even if someone does no longer actually like sure types of conversation, it could be clean to reply to them.

You might likely gather a message from a person who isn't always interested in you. If they refuse to speak with you on the cellphone, they may be rejecting you.

When they do now not reply, you need to leave a message. I would love to fulfill you as fast as possible. "Please, contact me".

Do not name "just to speak." This can also seem uncommon, and some people dislike talking at the telephone. Have a selected purpose in thoughts. You is probably calling to deliver out an invite or to inquire about something.

You ought to say some thing which includes, "I look at an commercial for that play you mentioned, do you need to transport collectively?"."

For the time being, refrain from contacting them. If you are not positive who normally begins a communique, take a second. Check to peer if they may get throughout to you without any strive from you. If they do, this is exceptional information. It's in all likelihood that they have located your absence and are lacking you. If they do no longer touch you, it is able to be because they did now not phrase or due to the reality they assumed you had already obtained the message.

If you've got got actual emotions for this individual, not staying in touch with them for a couple of months may be hard. But it's miles crucial this is finished to look when you have been omitted.

3. Direct Questioning.

Determine how you can method them. It's horrifying to ask a person straight away if they will be inquisitive about you. You may also additionally be part of up with them in person or speak with them thru text or email. Adopt a more to be had method.

Asking thru textual content or electronic mail, gives the alternative man or woman extra time to react without feeling forced. You will, but, need to be patient earlier than you get a response, which is probably nerve-wracking.

When you ask in person, you could get a direct respond, however the individual may additionally feel burdened. In a casual manner, inquire whether or not they will be interested. Even if you care about their friendship, don't display it.

Enquire in advance in a honest manner, and make it obvious that you're open to any reaction they provide. Maintain a low-stakes exchange. They may not care approximately you, but it speaks more approximately them than approximately you.

The first-rate component to do is ship them a textual content or e-mail that announces, "I cannot inform out of your messages if you're inquisitive about a meeting. If so, I would really like to set up a few element with you. "otherwise, no trouble."

Some folks would likely sincerely be too ashamed to admit they may be now not worried. If they declaration some thing alongside the ones lines, "I experience your commercial enterprise enterprise. I'm in fact engrossed" You might also moreover say, "Nice. So, please keep in touch on every occasion you want to loaf around."

You can speak approximately a few thing like on the same time as you notice "I take satisfaction in spending wonderful time with you, but it's miles been hard for me to determine in case you do as well. Can we talk approximately it?"

Gracefully reply. It's outstanding if the individual can display that they may be excited. Tell them you may not mind spending some time with them. If they will be no longer endorsed, allow them to recognise that you understand.

If you've got were given been refused, you could say something to the impact of, "Thank you for being so forthright with me. I genuinely choice we can also moreover stay buddies."

Asking them why they aren't interested by you is a bad idea. This need to make the alternative person enjoy uncomfortable.

Its great you glide on as soon as it's miles demonstrated which you've been rejected. At the stop of the day, it's far useful to have sufficient cash to be aware about a person that careless for you.

Chapter 9: What Constant Rejection Can Do To A Person?

Rejection is an inevitable detail of existence. Recognize that feeling of rejection and denial isn't bizarre the least bit. That's why we have got were given addressed your rejection problems so that you can resume getting your self out there with out worry.

1. What Happens while you're Continuously Rejected?

You in all likelihood grow to be angry. Any time you strive beginning a courting of some type (dating or friendship), choice can enjoy lost. In such an instance, you will possibly get angry at the individual that rejected you, or the sector round you. Its superb to be dissatisfied and you could employ that feeling to encourage you to keep going.

It must make you feel downhearted .Frequent acts of rejection can get on one's nerves. Studies have it that everyday instances of refusal can bring about despair. Early signs and signs and symptoms of melancholy are tiredness, not having the willingness to do something, or preserving yourself some distance from others.

You can emerge as green with envy of others. When humans close to you're normal rather than being rejected, it's far tough to control. It is not absolutely horrific to be green with envy of each other person, as Jealousy is a natural feeling.

2. What is Your Reaction to Constant Rejection?

Recognize your feelings. You also can revel in exhausted, sad, irritated, or insecure. It is ordinary to sense your emotions; you have nothing to do not forget. You can determine to talk topics over with a pal. The more you could allow stuff out, the higher you could enjoy due to the fact you could now not revel in obligated to hold your mind hidden.

Focus on the future. The reality that you've been refused before, is not a demonstration there may be a repeat of such. We have all expert our percentage of rejection in some unspecified time within the destiny in life. Your recognition have to be at the destiny and permit pass of the beyond.

Consider consulting a highbrow fitness professional. A therapist or counselor assist you to in processing your feelings in a healthy way. Book a session with an expert in highbrow fitness to percent your issues, in case you experience like you've got got been a sufferer of rejection your entire lifestyles. They'll be able to deliver an cause for why you're constantly being rejected and the manner to decorate your vanity so that you can located your self to be had all over again.

3. Is Regular Rejection Normal?

Yes, it's far a fairly not unusual human revel in to be rejected. We are all rejected in some unspecified time inside the future in our lives, whether or not or no longer romantic, platonic, or expert. It's understandable that not every body would like or approve human beings for who we are. The everyday refusal at one-of-a-kind time's shows which you've been going all out, that is a tremendous function to very very own.

four. Why Am I So Afraid of Rejection?

Rejection can bring about physical ache, which can be scary. Study after have a study has discovered out that social denial triggers the same factors of our brains as bodily ache. That sensation is unsightly, and it is not some thing you need to enjoy greater than as quick as. That's why rejection is so frightening—it could certainly be unstable.

Thankfully, the pain does not endure indefinitely. Time is the first rate medication, experts say, and as soon as the initial wonder has surpassed, your thoughts will speedy recover from the rejection.

five.What Does Frequent Rejection in a Relationship do to you?

It should make you sense much less assured. When you are being rejected with the useful resource of using your companion rejects, you may begin to nurture the feeling that they not like (or love) you. Even if it isn't correct, it may negatively have an impact on your vanity and make you revel in horrible. In this case, the first-rate trouble to do is sit down down and chat together along with your companion about why you enjoy undesirable and what you could every do to prevent it.

Strike up a communication with the beneficial resource of asking something in the line of, "Hey babe, are we in a position to speak? I've been feeling incredibly rejected currently, and I just idea to apprehend in on how topics are going with us."

You might also additionally withdraw from your relationship as a result of it. You also can determine to give up trying after being rejected in severa times, each emotionally or physical. This may motive you to retreat from your partner, which may be risky on your dating. This creates an great possibility so you can have an open speak collectively along with your companion.

Schedule a meeting with a pair's counselor if you're having issues speakme together collectively together with your associate or developing with a solution that works for both of you.

6. What is the Best Way to Avoid Taking Rejection Personally?

Give your self credit score for taking the hazard of getting your self available. Asking a person out or telling how a great deal you recognize the character isn't always an easy challenge, but you probably did it! Applaud yourself for taking the step, even though it didn't pop out precisely the manner you had hoped.

It can function a manner of mastering. Have you asked a person out too quick? Did you pass over the clues that they have been most effective searching out buddies? Try to keep in mind everything that happened as much as the rejection and use it as a coaching 2d for the future.

For instance, assume you asked someone out whom you had superb stated for some days. You can try to get to understand her higher next time in advance than asking her out.

Chapter 10: How To Deal With Family Rejection

One of the maximum hard things a person may match thru is own family rejection. It's herbal to revel in damage and loss in waves, and those are sensations that do not go away without trouble. If you're coping with family rejection, recollect that with the resource of the use of looking for strategies to manage, you've got taken a crucial first step in the route of recovery. You can do loads to artwork through your emotions, gather what you can't alternate, and emerge higher and stronger than before.

1. Give Yourself the Space to Analyze Your Emotions.

Accept your feelings and do no longer be worried to cry. Ignoring your feelings won't lead them to vanish, so confronting them head-on is your excellent wager. Listen to depression track, cry, and inform your self the way you surely experience. It's in no way smooth to be rejected via using manner of someone close to you, however even as it comes from a member of the family, it is made worse. Knowing that it's far all proper to confess you're unhappy ought to make the course to happiness masses much less complicated ultimately.

However, do not stay moody for too long. Put off the tune and take a stroll after being attentive to a few depression tunes. The feelings may not be all of sudden as you pass over this.

Realize that you have no effect over your own family's behavior, regardless of how tough it is. However, you could choose the way you react to it. To feel resilient after the grief technique, deal with your very very very own emotional health.

Understand that your own family's rejections do no longer have some thing to do at the side of your self esteem.

2. Write Down Your Feelings.

Writing down your feeling and offer you with more insights. Your own family's rejection can also make you revel in a number of feelings, together with despair, rage, and astonishment. Purchase a diary or notepad after which use it to record your emotions. Set aside time for reflections. As you write, you want to gain a higher facts of your feelings.

After the refusal, use the pocket e-book to enhance your arrogance. Family rejection is extraordinarily painful. Pen down all of the belongings you understand about your self to maintain it from bad your self-worth. Look thru your list the subsequent time you're feeling depressed!

Journaling may additionally furthermore assist you in recognizing triggers. Write right down to your notes the instances even as you were severely depressed. Consider what that they had in not unusual and the way you could make adjustments to prevent the ones triggers.

three. When You Are Low in Spirit, Repeat Positive Affirmations to Yourself.

Promise your self that you could overcome this impediment. Motivational expenses can characteristic the top notch method to lighten your soul. Use expressions like "I am an achiever," "I'm born to be brilliant," and "I am talented, I absolutely have the tendencies to triumph over any threats." Even if you doubt how beneficial this may be, saying this powerful phrase will assist you note your self and your situations in a more excessive fine perspective.

"I'm wonderfully made," and "I'm worthy of honor," are examples of motivational terms you've got to investigate to mention to yourself.

As lots as viable, avoid poor wondering. Don't permit thoughts like "I'm a awful individual" repeat themselves to your head. No don't forget how hard it might be to avoid such, attempt not to allow such thoughts dominate your mind. Reframe your thinking from a greater first rate mindset each time you find out yourself being particularly vital of your self. Replace horrible thoughts with high first-rate ones, which incorporates "I'll be happy once more." "This is mainly difficult, but I am assured that I will discover a few happiness over again inside the destiny!"

Negative notion may be a" killjoy" as it could make you pass over out at the first-rate topics in lifestyles.

Redefine the rejection as a useful experience. It can be higher so you can stay some distance from your family now, in particular when you have already been emotionally and bodily abused.

These moves may also have prolonged-term effects, and forgiving or reconnecting might not be solid. Remind yourself that you are more secure without the toxic or abusive family individuals on your life if you grew up in a unmarried. You can use their rejection as an possibility to surround your self with those who deal with you, admire you, and love you.

Concentrate on self-care. To get over rejection, cope with your self. Consume nutrient-dense substances. Get enough sleep (7-10 hours consistent with night time time) to enjoy cushty and prepared to stand the annoying conditions of each day. Take up new sports activities at the manner to growth your lifestyles, which includes studying to play an tool or stepping into a e-book membership. Even if you're dwelling with the sorrow of family alienation, all of these behavior make your lifestyles feel like it's far heading in the right course.

To sense higher, keep away from using pills or alcohol. They won't help you ultimately and may perhaps make you sense worse.

Look for close to ties in unique locations. Blood circle of relatives aren't the best circle of relatives individuals. Build near friendships and are attempting to find sympathetic and healthy romantic relationships. You want to surround yourself with people who make you revel in stable, valued, and supported. ! Be within the company of people who inspire self belief and arrogance.

If you used to love date nights at the aspect of your family, have a film night time time time at the side of your friends. You can also have dinner with buddies. Even a gaggle of near friends can spend the holidays collectively!

Consider volunteering for your area, joining a community ebook company, or contacting people on line to meet new human beings.

Be sincere with a person you remember approximately your emotions. To communicate with a chum, call them or walk over to their residence. Tell them about your situation and are searching for to get their recommendation or speak about your feelings with them. A genuine friend may additionally provide you with terms of encouragement and reassure you that you are loved and cared for via manner of others.

Talk to a professional in case you regardless of the reality that want assist expertise the way you enjoy after speakme on your buddies or in case you do now not apprehend whom to speak to. A therapist or counselor let you increase coping mechanisms. If your circle of relatives constantly disrespects you, set some boundaries.

Chances are you may despite the fact that be contacted once in a while with the beneficial useful resource of your family. Tell them that in the event that they address you badly, their actions are unacceptable. Be sure to let them recognize the manner you experience the subsequent time you enjoy uncomfortable. I cannot hold speakme if you method me like that," or "I do now not want to preserve this communication in case you method me like that." If they do now not trade their conduct, it can be time to prevent speaking with them on your private emotional well-being.

If you revel in uncomfortable with them or assume they do now not recognize your limits, you are free to prevent communicating with them. Social distancing, as tough as it is able to be, can be the high-quality selection in your bodily and intellectual fitness.

There is not any need to decide right away in case you aren't truly positive what you want. Determining your restriction is pinnacle to ensuring your safety and satisfaction.

four. Consult a Therapist or Counselor to move Through Your Feelings.

A expert can offer you with precise healing techniques. They can also offer you with an intention point of view, which a relied on friend or own family won't be able to provide. Find an expert family divorce expert to help you manage your feelings.

Finding the ideal therapist or counselor can occasionally take some time. Don't be discouraged if the first one you be aware does not look correct on you. Find each exceptional professional on your region who will let you higher!

Chapter 11: Supporting A Chum Who Grow To Be Rejected

Even at the same time as rejection is a easy human emotion, it can be excruciatingly painful. If a pal is going through the rejection segment, you may consolation her with the useful useful resource of patiently listening and supporting in placing her rejection into context. Rejection can be disheartening for optimum humans; knowing the early symptoms and signs and symptoms and signs and symptoms of melancholy will pass an extended manner that will help you higher assist your pal as he struggles to govern.

1. Being an Effective Listener.

If your opinion hasn't been requested, do now not say it. If your buddy has just been rejected, he may not need to pay interest what he could do in a unique manner subsequent time. Even even though her actions can also moreover have contributed to her rejection or a lack of a system or a dating, an unsolicited belief at this aspect may not be appropriate for her.

Now isn't the time to remind your pal of her beyond response to dropping her undertaking or her boyfriend.

The high-quality way you may assist your buddy to get through this tough time is by manner of being a excellent listener, irrespective of the situation. You may also moreover need to provide a slight concept for your pal if she asks on your assist in figuring out what she's doing wrong.

Assist your pal in rephrasing the rejection. You should now not want to overemphasize the "opportunities for growth" that consists of rejection, however you could moreover assist your friend to trying to find tactics to benefit from the incident. In each hassle, there may be always a silver lining. Occasionally you could want the assist of a friend to apprehend it.

Not getting the approach she supposed should purchase her time to wait that family revel in she changed into looking forward to.

Being unmarried gives you with greater flexibility.

Replicate your pal's emotions. Helping your friend address her struggling is one manner to show your guide. Inquire about her feelings and reassure her that they may be normal. It will make her feel higher information she has a friend whom she could be capable of percentage her painful revel in with, with out being rejected.

"It seems like you are very broken up approximately subjects," as an example, ought to make him experience supported.

Prepare to stay silent. If your friend changed into honestly hurt thru the rejections, she might not be capable of specific her emotions. She have to actually want to take a seat down with you silently. It will suffice in case you are present and willing to pay interest whilst she is prepared to speak. A warmness consist of can do the magic.

Other strategies to offer guide to a chum who isn't geared up to talk approximately her feelings but, encompass chatting approximately some element aside from the rejection or finishing an interest collectively. Engage in a laugh sports collectively.

2. Setting the Rejection in its Rightful Place.

Give your friend kudos for attempting. Rejection is an unavoidable impact of doing some thing new and volatile.

Even if it did no longer schooling session in the end—the man stopped calling, she did now not win the element within the play, she wasn't supplied a merchandising—she merits credit rating for trying.

It may be useful to remind them that they threat being rejected. Because rejection letters are so ubiquitous, authors, as an example, automatically cowl their partitions with them. Thousands of refusal slips are furnished within the life of a well-known author in advance than their paintings is time-commemorated for e-book.

You can tell her to attempt all over again if she does now not get the mission offer this time if the denial modified into for a few issue with a low possibility of rejection - which includes a activity offer as an example.

Tell your friend that rejection takes area all of the time. After all, sincerely all people suffers rejection in a few unspecified time inside the destiny all through their lives. Going out for the group, using to universities, attempting to land an extraordinary venture, or asking out the individual you have been crushing on all summer season are all strategies to get rejected.

Although each rejection feels personal, it is commonly just a rely of terrible timing.

No one is evidence towards rejection, regardless of how clever, humorous or gifted they may be. If it helps, check at others who've in the end succeeded and examine how many rejections they faced.

Consider speaking approximately your very personal reviews with rejection. Telling your friend she isn't always the outstanding one experiencing rejection might be useful to her.

Discussing your non-public rejections — the roles you have got got been dismissed from, rejection notices you've got were given gotten, failed romances — can also need to make your pal sense more comfortable and much less on my own.

At the identical time, hold in mind that your friend's revel in can also vary considerably from yours. Don't brag about yourself or profess to apprehend how your buddy is feeling.

Never encourage a chum through the use of pronouncing, "You will..." or "You need to..." Although the ones remarks also can look like encouraging, they will be probably to be misinterpreted via someone managing rejection.

Instead, describe the manner you dealt with a situation of rejection similar to that of your friend, then say that everybody handles rejection in a high-quality manner.

Discuss your friend's excessive excellent developments. While your female friend's talents can also require some paintings, she moreover has many fantastic characteristics. Remind her of the capabilities that others admire in her. Give clean examples that she can not disprove.

Remind your pal that her terrific sense of humor after developing a darkish comic tale approximately her situation can assist her see the truth approximately what you are saying.

Don't overdo it with compliments or say assets you do no longer in reality be given as genuine with. Your pal will come across your deception.

Keeping your buddy hopeful won't assist. Accepting the rejection will help your pal in transferring on to the following degree of his lifestyles.

Nobody is privy to what the destiny holds. Your name can be advise for the interest if the person who were given the hobby says no. Or in all likelihood his ex will rethink. But hoping for important changes is neither viable nor properly timed.

Help your friend understand that rejection isn't private. Rejection is a commonplace revel in and we have were given got little control over it. Realize that you may not like anybody you've got got interplay with and we won't get all the jobs we're searching out.

Encourage your friend to discover someone who will show her the identical emotion.

Point out a tremendous element she has presently accomplished.

Look for strategies to cheer her up. What have been a number of your buddy's preferred activities before the rejection? Make time for each one-of-a-kind thru looking sporting activities or going to the movies together.

Your acquaintance might also furthermore undergo financially if the refusal outcomes in a lack of profits. Be careful not to interact in luxurious sports activities as this will have unfavorable outcomes.

Avoid challenge activities if you want to remind her of her past experience.

3. Look for Depression Symptoms.

Keep a watch out for any giant shifts in behavior. Getting without problems indignant over every small trouble or being surprisingly moody are some of the symptoms and signs of despair. Sleep adjustments, which encompass napping too much or now not sound asleep the least bit, can suggest depression.

She might not be herself even after she overcomes the rejection.

She can also lose interest in subjects that she as soon as loved.

Death has piqued your hobby. Pay hobby in case your friend begins speakme about loss of lifestyles and lack of life. Even if uttered gently, phrases like "I may as well be useless" or "Why do not I really give up it all and set all and sundry out in their distress" can advocate suicidal dispositions.

Have an open communique at the aspect of your girlfriend if you be aware that she is susceptible to harming herself (or others). Just ask her if she has any mind about harming herself. Most probable she'll deny it, however that can be an avenue for her to talk and pour out her coronary heart to you.

If you trust she is affected by a catastrophe or in chance, name for help.

Urge her to are looking for help. Chances are, your pal will not recover from the pain of anxiety and despair with out proper remedy.

Make it acknowledged to her which you're available to help her in booking an appointment or displaying up at a assist agency.

Remember you can not strain her to look a therapist. If she would not want remedy, reassure her which you're there to help her.

Keep an eye fixed fixed fixed out for suicide warning signs and symptoms. All too frequently, caution signs and symptoms of suicide are nice visible in hindsight, but they will be instead commonplace. If your friend has untreated depression after her rejection, she can be having suicidal thoughts. Contact a scientific expert or a counselor as quickly as you word an increase in any of the signs and symptoms underneath, or name an emergency quantity proper away assist.

Obtaining the system to commit suicide, which incorporates storing drugs (for an overdose) or buying a gun, are a few caution indicators.

Increased drug or alcohol consumption.

Giving away one's possessions or dashing to get one's affairs in order even as there may be no apparent purpose to.

Taking highly volatile or self-detrimental moves

Distinguishing adjustments, or tension, mainly at the same time as they're decided by way of the use of manner of some of the opposite symptoms referred to right right right here.

Chapter 12: How To Overcome Your Fear Of Rejection

You've submitted an software program to the college of your goals... You've proposed in your weigh down... You've performed for the pastime of your dreams... And had been grew to come to be down. Even the most successful human beings are trouble to rejection. Trying some component new may consequences in rejection. What counts, in the end, is the manner you cope with the rejection. Do you preserve trying or are you usually scared of being rejected?

The worry of rejection can keep you from attempting new things and going in advance. Fortunately, there are numerous strategies for managing rejection and growing your self-self assure such which you not dread rejection and as a substitute see it as an opportunity.

Understanding How to Deal with Rejection

Maintain your composure and common experience. Having a way will assist you in analyzing to overcome your fear of rejection.

In addition, it is a exquisite way to enhance yourself-self assurance. We are thru and large pushed by using the usage of emotions inside the second in location of our brains. You might also additionally refocus your fear so you reply sensibly and successfully if you can stay calm.

It's all too tempting to permit your initial reaction to a horrible state of affairs control you. If you expect to be rejected, plan in advance right away!

Begin through the usage of preserving a mag. Because it allows you to record your issues, doubts, feelings, mind, and thoughts, journaling can be relatively appropriate for cognitive mirrored photo and improvement. Putting your feelings down let you release them, and will prevent you from residing on things you can't exchange (like a breakup, rejection letter from the university, failed scholarship software program, and so forth). For letting pass of your fears, writing may be an powerful device.

Putting sentiments and unstructured mind into phrases can can help you understand subjects better. Jotting about your fears motives you to recollect why you are afraid.

You won't need to percent your diaries with honestly everyone, and you may always re-have a study an event in a while in case you experience irrational or juvenile.

Determine if you have an "all-or-now not something" mentality. It is "all-or-now not some thing" or "black-and-white" questioning whilst you assert: "I might not skip everywhere" or "This is the fine college for me." These statements can intensify the danger of rejection. How are you able to save you it? Here are a few ideas.

Put together a listing of "all-or-not anything" statements you might imagine of.

Concentrate at the remarkable. For instance, "I'll look for some distinct manner. I now have an terrific cover letter as a result of the usage of for this assignment.

Always remember that rejection is a opportunity. Rejection is a part of normal lifestyles, and dealing with your worry requires expertise that it could take location, that it does to hundreds of humans, and that it is not the stop, however instead the start. Have you ever carried out for a way? So do one hundred one in all a kind parents. On a date, you ask a person out? The reaction want to either be a Yes or a No.

You are simplest in fee of yourself. You haven't any control over the splendid of the alternative scholarship programs if you have a take a look at for one. You can top notch do your fantastic!

Remember that rejection receives much less tough with exercising. It hurts, but the greater you cope with it, the easier it'll get.

Accept the rejection with grace. Accepting rejection gently has continually been the satisfactory way to move, even though it's some distance much less hard stated than completed. Show compassion and empathy in vicinity of lashing out. You moreover have to have one issue in time rejected someone; this ought to provide you with an concept of methods it feels to interrupt someone's coronary heart. Moreover, you can no longer want to bear as a bargain emotional pressure like lash out at someone.

After receiving a rejected technique software program program, thank the interviewer for their time with an email.

Emails together with the ones will help you permit move of unwanted emotions or thoughts, and they may furthermore help you find out what wants to be advanced.

Keep your bearings. You might be denied a few possibilities, but now not all. If you don't located your self available, you may no longer be capable of advantage your goals and goals. Because you start putting your self to be had and attempting, you may anticipate some rejection on occasion. But it truely is still development! It's essential to hold a larger mind-set that extends beyond the at once of rejection.

If you are feeling beaten through a state of affairs in that you've been grew to emerge as down, remind yourself, "Will this be a trouble subsequent week? What about the subsequent year?"

You must be relieved if the solutions to those questions are "likely no longer."

Recognize that occurrences are impartial except you assign them a experience. You need no longer problem your self over a scenario that has no longer but occurred. We regularly presume a right away hyperlink amongst our feelings and the contemporary incidence. It's essential to bear in mind that rejection in truth shows you did not achieve what you desired. You add next sentiments of doubt, fear, inadequacy, or depression. Try to be aware whilst you feature strong feelings to a impartial scenario.

It's critical which you try to figure out both what the rejection manner objectively and the emotions you are ascribing to it.

For instance, "This characteristic turn out to be have end up down. This rejection motives me to mistrust my very very very own ability. My sadness stems from the fact that I emerge as confident I become nicely certified."

Analyzing the feelings you feature to the scenario can assist in higher information your private feelings and uncertainties, which you may address within the levels that observe.

Chapter 13: Seeing Rejection As An Advantage

Consider rejection as a present day-day possibility. Rejection may be taken into consideration as an advantage; it all relies upon on your attitude. A interest rejection results in more opportunities. Although it could no longer seem so at the time of the rejection, you can find out your self questioning, "Thank god, I did no longer get that hobby!" inside the destiny.

Consider this example: you're looking for a system possibility. It can also even name for all your time, despite the fact that the enterprise enterprise gives huge advantages in phrases of income and experience.

Your personal lifestyles isn't any first rate. Would you recollect courting a new lady after being rejected by way of way of a lady you favored?

Take rejection as a mastering revel in. Rejection is a place to begin, now not an quit.

See rejection as an avenue for boom in area of fearing it.

Handling out an invite to an individual in man or woman is extra desired than sending a text message.

You decided to double-test your artwork if you did no longer get the procedure because of the reality your resume had mistakes!

Attempt some extra. In phrases of natural opportunity, the greater times you positioned your self available and strive, the more likely it's far to expose out. Know that now not whatever adjustments if you do not strive. The quality way to be successful is to disregard rejection.

If you isolate yourself, possibilities are you'll never get a "sure." Although rejection is painful, each rejection brings you toward your motive!

Consider your alternatives. We often assume we're being rejected due to our shortcomings. It's essential to realise that there are constantly elements and records you don't know about, and there can be different reasons why a person rejected you. If you start to lose your cool, realize that you can not understand the whole thing, and there is probably other reasons why you failed to be triumphant.

You can be rejected from a graduate school due to the fact an applicant with interior connections took your vicinity.

You aren't the reason of every rejection you revel in, so take it easy on yourself.

Your scenario does do not outline your Worth. What people say about you, isn't always your industrial organization, and do not make it yours. You is probably strong sufficient to deal with any rejection if you broaden and keep self-self warranty. Read books, take a route, look at a talent, and permit your attention be channeled in the course of developing your thoughts. You will gain extra arrogance if you frequently engage in mind-developing activities.

Do now not appearance to others for validation of your values, as this is the deliver of your worry of rejection. You are by myself responsible to yourself.

Remember your strengths. We become greater at risk of the concern of rejection if we experience unsettled and whilst our feelings of self esteem are relying on others. It's crucial that you are feeling satisfied with and assured in your self, further to respect your capabilities. The first step closer to locating self guarantee that comes from interior in preference to from outside is to hold in thoughts and report your capabilities.

Write down your capabilities and talents for your pocket ebook to growth your vanity and combat any doubts that rise up even as you worry rejection.

Make a list of your accomplishments. Have you ever finished a marathon? Have you gained a massive scholarship? Did you assist a missing child in locating their dad and mom? This will help you benefit self-guarantee.

Concentrate in your desires. Create a list of goals or assets you want to art work inside the direction of, based completely at the trends you have absolutely located. It may assist you revel in extra confident and fulfilled. Consider this: How will I skip approximately accomplishing the ones goals? What need to be finished? What steps can I take right now? Planning, wearing out, and undertaking dreams will make you experience greater strong in your destiny opportunities and much less fearful of rejection.

You can advantage self perception through breaking down your dreams into smaller steps. Furthermore, fulfillment in the ones minor ranges can assist shield rejection's influences.

Make a listing of what you need to do within the future to boom your chances. You'll benefit self notion as you entire each of those little dreams.

Think approximately your tremendous contributions to the arena. Helping and offering for others is surprisingly exciting and offers you a sense of duty. Self-self perception and vanity are substantially extra suitable by means of manner of using this revel in of reason.

For instance, volunteering has been tested to beautify important regions of human well-being, which incorporates optimism, lifestyles delight, conceitedness, a feel of manage over one's lifestyles, and physical fitness.

You can favor to function a volunteer every in a university or health center occasion. If you choose animals, there is continually the selection of volunteering at a humane society.

Treat others with kindness and generosity. Being type to others, even strangers, makes them revel in accurate, which makes you feel relevant, and so forth.

Be innovative and take movement. Set aside time every day to do some thing you adore, be it reading, cooking, gardening, or gambling video games. Take benefit of the time you've got set aside; you have earned it. As wished, repeat that statement. Enhancing your existence with sports activities you experience makes you revel in better about yourself and thus extra able to confront life's problems and private issues, together with rejection.

Try some detail superb. Take a language splendor, a cooking elegance, or an advanced elegance. Analyzing new sports can display competencies or skills that you did not understand before.

This can growth your arrogance and self esteem, in addition to open up new possibilities in your lifestyles that you had now not even taken into consideration previously.

You'll help support your resistance to rejection if you can strive some aspect new and cope with your worries.

Look after yourself. Investing effort and time into your emotional and physical nicely-being assist you to revel in more self-confident. The more healthy your thoughts and body are, the much more likely you are to be content material fabric with yourself and to efficiently deal with the risk of rejection. Self-care consists of doing all your exquisite to stay wholesome, a few element which means that to you. Here are some hints:

Take proper care of your frame. Make positive you eat nutritious, unprocessed factors, loosen up and sleep sufficient (at least 7-eight hours).

It is likewise crucial to workout. Exercising has been located in research to beautify conceitedness.

Allow your self to unwind. Stress is a big problem that plenty parents face, and it may serve to expand and enlarge terrible feelings and concerns.

Set aside time for rest to help you deal with pressure in your every day lifestyles.

Chapter 14: Dealing With Professional Rejection

Start small, but smart. Taking professional dangers may be scary, and consequently difficult to encourage yourself to carry out. It's beneficial to hold in mind that, just like Rome wasn't built in a day, your profession might not surge or collapse following a unmarried triumph or setback. Prepare yourself for the long time through the usage of taking little movements at the begin.

If you are seeking out a new career, as an example, join up for a connecting birthday celebration or an alumni meet up earlier than you start sending out your applications and doing interviews.

If you want to increase your chances of having a advertising, ask for and acquire more responsibility at paintings. If you're in advance about your desire to increase within the agency, the utility and interview method will pass masses greater with out trouble.

Inquire of educators and coworkers for candid reviews. Try to create an surroundings among your pals and coworkers, wherein you supply each unique actual and thorough remarks on your efforts. You're practicing the auditory senses and processing evaluations that are not unambiguously accurate, even in case you're now not rejecting each top notch's work outright.

Consider the results. What's the worst that can end cease result from a rejection? It is common for rejection to appear more essential than it genuinely is due to the depth of the worry. After a few idea, you'll find out that the real-life consequences of receiving a professional rejection aren't nearly as awful as you had feared: no matter how horrible it hurts, it's not the cease of the sector.

Try to assume the worst-case situation. This may additionally additionally moreover appear horrifying inside the beginning, but if you pursue the story to its logical cease, you could find out that not receiving the hobby or promoting become not a existence or demise situation.

Don't without a doubt disregard it. The best way to conquer the ache related to rejection is to tell your self that it is the other individual's loss, not yours. However, disregarding it on this manner prevents you from absolutely exploiting the hazard and gaining new know-how. Instead of discarding the experience, don't forget how you could apply it to better your self and your efforts.

Feel free to solicit constructive comments from an interviewer. It's no longer out of location to ask questions, although there may be no response. Their complaint will give you large perception into the interviewer's angle, which you could use to beautify your software documents and interview technique inside the destiny.

Make a pleasant out of it. After rejection, it's far herbal to feel depressed, but you could distract yourself thru doing some component outstanding. Utilize a publishing house denial to beautify your writing abilties, or use a system or college rejection to enhance your subsequent software.

It may be useful to remind yourself of what you have got were given control over and what you do not. You don't have any manipulate over whether or not or not or no longer or no longer you're rejected, but you do have manipulate over how you respond to it. Instead of thinking about what occurred, recognition on your personal behavior and your reactions to the rejection.

It is probably beneficial to remind yourself of what you could and cannot manage. You haven't any manipulate over whether or not or now not or not you are rejected, however you could manipulate the way you respond to it. Rather than spending time mulling over the incident, recognition on your non-public attitude and reaction to the rejection.

Chapter 15: Why People Leave Us

proper right here are numerous motives why the Lord will allow people to leave you and sometimes even harm you. Abraham is a great example of this. God instructed him to break up himself from his circle of relatives and bypass on an extended journey to an undefined Promised Land. Abraham emerge as to move away what he come to be acquainted with to what he became sudden with. I take shipping of as genuine with God does this to teach our individual and convey us to a place of solitude to train us a few essential topics.

The Lord had said to Abram, "Go from your u . S . A ., your humans and your father's household to the land I will show you. Genesis 12:1

Abraham encountered numerous instances of rejection and betrayals in this new journey.

1.	He encountered battle collectively alongside together with his relative Lot.

2.   He had to fight a war on behalf of his relative Lot. (Genesis 14:1-sixteen)

3.   Abraham became continuously rescuing Lot.

four.   Someone may also say, in which have become God in severa those? I suggest, how will you undergo a lot battle with one precise member of the family?

This is what I name cycles of conflict with loved ones. I even have determined out that in lifestyles, you just can't please positive human beings. Perhaps you're nevertheless forcing a courting that you see genuinely has run its path. Maybe sure humans's season in your lifestyles has ended and you don't apprehend the way to leave such relationships.

Thank God that they rejected you. It modified into God's mercy and His way that brought about them to go away you. You can also moreover bypass over them but recognize that the Lord allowed them to go away you because of the truth their time to your lifestyles had ended.

Another way to test rejection is that the Lord allowed human beings to depart you due to the truth he preferred to humble you. I without a doubt have had that revel in over and over all yet again, in which I had been abandoned, abandoned or obtained unexpected resignations from my company. Although every departure is disappointing and leaves within the again of severa questions, once I subsequently mirror on the state of affairs, I realize God desired to train me to now not depend on people but rely upon Him by myself.

The reality is that for plenty humans, it is their personal companion and kids that abandon them. This can be a superb embarrassment when people comprehend that your own family members do no longer aid you. If that takes region to you, you could endure in thoughts it as God humbling you even though the process.

There also are times while humans depart you because your future does now not encompass them. When God desires you to in truth see His glory for your life, He gets rid of humans as a way to carry you to His motive. Not anyone is called to be a part of your group or adventure.

Rejection Hurts

Rejection, abuse, insults, ache, betrayal, disappointments, decisions, and complaint, reason us ache. Emotional pain is regularly greater devastating than physical pain. Emotional pain is damage that originates from non-bodily property. Sometimes, this emotional distress is the give up give up result of the actions of others.

Rejection hurts.

Other times, it is probably the end end result of remorse, grief, or loss. In first rate instances, it's miles a case of not feeling favored thru others. No remember what the cause is, this intellectual pain can be excessive and therefore appreciably have an effect on many particular regions of your lifestyles. Of all the emotional wounds we go through in existence, I assume rejection is possibly the most not unusual and maximum common one humans undergo.

By the time we acquire High School we've been grew to become down from attending birthday activities, out of location a scholar council election, excluded from attending well-known events, dropped thru friends with out explanation or been bullied.

We manage to get through the ones years only to be faced with a present day-day set of rejections in the subsequent segment of our lives. We get grew to come to be down through way of capability dates, we don't get the method we've were given prepared and planned for, and we live snubbed with the beneficial resource of capability friends.

As we grow old we realize that our neighbours are giving us the bloodless shoulderand on occasion unluckily enough our households close us off.

Rejection cuts deep.

Rejection cuts deep; it scrapes and tears our emotional pores and pores and skin apart. Some rejections are so excessive that they depart an prolonged-lasting impact on one's feelings and life. I honestly have discovered that many human beings underestimate the pain of rejection, the ache of feeling undesirable and the pain of being ignored deliberately.

Rejection

The word rejection comes from a Latin phrase this means that that 'to be thrown lower back'. When we revel in rejection, the sensation no longer handiest stops us in our gift pastimes, however it from time to time motives us to retreat. Thus, in desire to progressing, we retrogress because of the concern of failure within the destiny.

There have become a time in my lifestyles when I had extra ache and damage than I need to rely. I changed into continually afraid definitely the worst could seem. I worried approximately why human beings deliberately favored to harm others. As a quit result, I couldn't enjoy my existence or have the peace God favored to offer me.

When you're going through hard times, which encompass rejection, you are not by myself. It is so crucial to maintain in mind that God is right there with you, and you may recall Him to help you thru it.

God by no means promised us a trouble-free existence, however He does promise to in no way depart us or forsake us.

God in no way promised us a trouble-unfastened lifestyles, but He does promise to in no way go away us or forsake us.

"Because God has said, "Never will I depart you, in no way will I forsake you." Hebrews 13:five

In tough instances, we're capable of take consolation information that He loves us extensively. He has His eye on us, and He is already jogging behind the scenes to assist us.

"But the eyes of the Lord are on folks who worry him, on those whose desire is in his unfailing love."

Psalm 33:18

Most of the rejections that we revel in range on multiple ranges. Some rejections are moderate and the emotional harm heals with time. However, even as left untreated, they become scars and purpose deeper ache in a unmarried's life. Experiencing profound or repeated rejection is pretty dangerous in your highbrow nicely-being.

One of the essential truths is that people need to experience well-known with the aid of others. When the need to belong isn't pleased because of rejection, it can have a effective negative effect on our walk with God. We begin to see God the identical manner we see the folks who rejected us but that ought to now not be the case. The Bible says, "There is not any fear in love. But best love drives out fear..." (1 John four:18)

Understanding God's love is the antidote to fear! God needs us to understand just how an entire lot He loves us and desires to help us.

There is not any fear in love. But great love drives out worry.

God created us to be social. If we're sincere, anybody care whether or not or not or not or no longer humans like us. The feeling of affection, affection, and belonging is vital for building our social lives and vast networks.

David Experienced Rejection

In the Bible, we see an example where David expert rejection. Fortunately, you're no longer the first-class individual who's needed to address this problem. After David modified into anointed because the destiny king of Israel, Saul have come to be his sour enemy.

Like David, anyone at one time or a few other address people who don't like us. Perhaps you've got folks that want to do you harm and notice you fail. This is wherein David positioned himself in 1 samuel 24.

His enemy, Saul, wanted to look him useless, and he spent a big quantity of time chasing David to kill him. Then in the future, Saul made a mistake. He walked right into the vicinity in which David and his guys have been with out understanding David become there. Imagine how you would probable have felt in case your worst enemy (or hater) have become in the the the front of you and didn't apprehend you were there. Would you attack that man or woman?

Most oldsters could not suppose twice about getting revenge on that man or woman, especially in view that doing so ought to signify we might not want to run and cover from them. However, David changed into distinct. Even in spite of the fact that David preferred to save you taking walks and hiding, he favored to honor God more. Saul turned into a king that God anointed, and David knew that he couldn't clearly kill him. Understanding this, he rejected thoughts to kill Saul.

Satan uses the impact of rejection to attack you

Rejection is one of the primary weapons Satan uses to keep us from transferring forward and playing the good life God has for us. Particularly, even as a few trouble bad takes region, the enemy dreams us to focus on all the "what ifs" and fill our lives with fear and anxiety. He desires to pull our focus far from God's love and faithfulness.

Hebrews 13:five-6 (AMP) is one in every of my desired passages of Scripture. Just observe what God says approximately you: "...I will in no way [under any circumstances] barren area you [nor provide you with up nor depart you with out assist, nor will I in any diploma leave you helpless, nor will I forsake or can help you down or lighten up My preserve on you [assuredly not]!

Some human beings have such tough existence instances that pleasurable their want to belong can gift a chief challenge. When we attempt simply hard for a few trouble, handiest to return face to face with a stable wall blockading us from feeling a enjoy of belonging, that may be heartbreaking. And the sensation of rejection that comes with that sting can be very discomforting; a feel of worthlessness, awkwardness, self-focus, unease, pain, shame, humiliation, distress and occasionally loss of self guarantee.

Jesus can heal your damaged coronary coronary heart

If you've got were given ever been confronted with rejection, Jesus desires to heal you. Don't count on that Jesus does now not apprehend the manner it seems like to be rejected.

1.   Matthew 21:forty , Acts 4:11 and Mark 12:10 talk of Jesus because the cornerstone which the developers rejected.

2.   1 Peter 2:7 discusses the rejection of Jesus. This references comparable wording in Psalm 118:22: The stone which the builders rejected has grow to be the chief cornerstone.

three.   According to Luke nine:fifty one-fifty six, on the same time as Jesus entered a Samaritan village, He have become not welcomed, because of the reality he become going on to Jerusalem. (There became enmity a number of the Jews and their temple in Jerusalem and Samaritans and their temple on Mount Gerizim) His disciples preferred to call down fireplace from heaven at the village however Jesus reprimanded them and they persevered on to every other village.

four.   John 6:60-sixty six records "many disciples" leaving Jesus after He stated that those who devour His body and drink His blood will live in Him and characteristic eternal lifestyles (John 6:48-fifty nine).

5.   In John 6:67-seventy one, Jesus asks the Twelve Apostles if similarly they need to move away, however Peter responds that they have turn out to be believers.

6.   Ultimately Jesus's very personal disciple Peter rejected Him. All 4 Gospels report an episode of the Apostle Peter denying Jesus 3 times at the night time of Christ's betrayal inside the courtyard of the excessive priest.

Jesus can heal you everywhere it hurts along side the pain of rejection.

Jesus can heal you anywhere it hurts which includes the rejection you have got persevered from people. The root motive of disapproval is thought greater thru Jesus than sincerely every person else. The Bible tells us Jesus came to heal all our wounds and broken hearts. His desire is to present you beauty in region of ashes and replace disappointment and mourning with the oil of Joy.

The Spirit of the Sovereign Lord is on me, due to the truth the Lord has anointed me to proclaim suitable information to the poor. He has sent me to bind up the brokenhearted, to proclaim freedom for the captives and launch from darkness for the prisoners, to proclaim the year of the Lord's pick out out and the day of vengeance of our God, to consolation all who mourn, and provide for folks who grieve in Zionto bestow on them a crown of beauty in area of ashes the oil of satisfaction, in preference to mourning, and a garment of praise in vicinity of a spirit of melancholy.

"They can be called o.K. Of righteousness, a planting of the Lord for the display of his beauty."

Isaiah 61:1-3

Jesus is familiar with what you're going thru because of the reality he come to be rejected with the aid of the usage of human beings in a few unspecified time in the destiny of his ministry who left while matters started out getting tough. (Read John 6:sixty seven, John 16:32) Jesus suffered the very last enjoy of abandonment and rejection on the identical time as loss of life on the skip. The Bible says, "About the ninth hour Jesus cried out in a loud voice, 'My God, my God, why have you ever ever ever forsaken me?" (Matthew 27:forty six NIV) Jesus is privy to what it seems like to be abandoned. He is aware the manner you experience. He is prepared to assist.

Prayer

Dear Jesus, I come to you nowadays because of the fact you recognize how horrible it feels to be abandoned and rejected with the beneficial resource of others. I now lay earlier than you what has passed off to me.

Jesus, I deliver my emotions in advance than you these days. Here are a number of the techniques I am feeling:

Hurt

Betrayed

Angry

Defeated

Unloved

Unlovable

Rejected

Defeated

Lonely

Isolated

Jesus, I thank you that you understand all of my emotions and that you hurt once I harm. I location my feelings and myself into your loving care. I want your comfort and treatment. I need to sense hopeful and entire over again in Jesus call!

I declare the subsequent ensures from the Bible over myself:

1.   "God has said, 'Never will I leave you; never will I forsake you.' So we say with self guarantee, 'The Lord is my helper; I will no longer be afraid. What can guy do to me?'" (Hebrews 13 5,6 NIV)

2.   "Be strong and brave. Do not be afraid or terrified due to them, for the Lord your God is going with you;

he will never leave you nor forsake you." (Deuteronomy 31:6 NIV)

3.   "And I will ask the Father, and he will offer you with a few different Counselor to be with you all the time – the Spirit of fact… But you recognize him, for he lives with you and may be in you." (John 14:sixteen,17 NIV)

4.   "I will not leave you as orphans; I will come to you." (John 14:sixteen)

five.   "Yea despite the fact that I stroll in the valley of the shadow of demise, I will worry no evil for thou paintings with me." (Psalm 23:four)

Chapter 16: The Mental Effect Of Rejection

Rejection can arise in numerous conditions. Regularly, dismissal portrays an example of an person or substance using someone or element away or out.

In the field of emotional nicely-being care, rejection most often alludes to the sensations of shame, trouble, or despondency human beings enjoy when they will be not mentioned through others. An character might also additionally need to experience neglected after big high-quality cuts off a friendship. A toddler who has no longer many or no partners would possibly enjoy rejected with the useful resource of peers. A man or woman who changed into surrendered for reception may additionally additionally moreover likewise stumble upon sensations of rejection.

Rejection can likewise give up result from life changing conditions not together with connections, as an example, being became down for a truely perfect situation at artwork or getting a dismissal letter from a faculty. While any dismissal may be difficult, some occurrences of rejection might be extra high-quality than others. Since maximum people want social contact, and many people pain for acknowledgment from society, being disregarded may have an effect on pessimistic sentiments and feelings.

(NOTE: Wherever you encounter the term DISMISSAL, it's far used alternatively or alternative for REJECTION)

The sensation of dismissal is familiar to have created as a transformative device to warning early those who have been in threat of being averted from the prolonged own family they had an area with. A hard dismissal from others inside the clan end up in all likelihood going to induce a person to trade any risky conduct to keep away from greater dismissal, or segregation, from the extended own family. The those who had the choice to avoid extra dismissal were certain to get via way of, at the same time as the folks who didn't view dismissal as specially excruciating may not have revised the culpable way of behaving, making them a good deal much less willing to get with the resource of. Along those lines, humans would possibly possibly have advanced to encounter dismissal as excruciating.

Today, many human beings disengage themselves or avoid associating with others at the same time as you remember that they're concerned about being dismissed. Apprehension approximately or aversion to dismissal that makes any character pull away from others can activate continual sensations of forlornness and sorrow. While dismissal interest can co-appear with numerous highbrow well-being troubles together with social anxiousness, avoidant character, and marginal character, it's some thing however an expert strength of will.

Dismissal interest is ordinary in masses of individuals with attention deficiency hyperactivity jumble (ADHD). Apprehension approximately rejection may also take location so mechanically in human beings with ADHD that some allude to it as dismissal delicate dysphoria. A few everyday signs of rejection sensitive dysphoria in people with ADHD encompass self-evaluation, anxiety in excellent times, and outrageous hassle after an apparent dismissal.

Impacts of Rejection on Brain Research

Rejection can be relatively agonizing considering it'd purpose humans to revel in as notwithstanding the truth that they'll be no longer wished, esteemed, or said. Most people will stumble upon rejection now or inside the future because it has to do with their lives. A teen may additionally enjoy rejected in quick thru the use of a bustling dad or mum, or an understudy could possibly feel a curt or inconsiderate. These types of rejection also can decide and are an awful lot a lot much less willing to make long lasting influences.

Continuous or prolonged haul dismissal might also have profound and enduring intellectual affects which might probably embody:

Injury: Long haul rejection or rejection that consequences in outrageous sentiments can also add to damage and may have critical highbrow results. For example, children who enjoy reliably brushed off via their dad and mom may probable find out it difficult to be successful at school and in institutions with their pals. A few people foster a steady feeling of dread in the direction of dismissal, often due to numerous horrendous encounters with rejection from the get-glide in the course of normal lifestyles.

Melancholy: Rejection has been associated with the development of distress in excessive student extra youthful girls;

however, distinctive individuals who experience rejection may likewise grow to be discouraged. Further, tormenting, which is basically a mixture of shunning and dismissal, can make numerous damaging results, including despondency, pressure, nutritional issues, and self-hurting strategies of behaving.

Torment Reaction: Exploration has proven that the mind solutions social soreness in a way this is just like the way that it answers actual torment. As per research, the very cerebrum pathways that are initiated via way of real torment are likewise actuated thru satisfactory pain, or dismissal. Receptor frameworks within the cerebrum moreover discharge everyday ache relievers (narcotics) even as a novel encounters social torment, equal to at the equal time as actual suffering is succesful.

Tension and Stress: Rejection have to regularly upload to prior situations like strain and uneasiness or result in their flip of occasions. Additionally, those and exceptional mental properly-being conditions can intensify sensations of dismissal.

Misuse: That's what one studies positioned, inside the male individuals from the assessment, the execution of maltreatment in close to connections have become related to the enjoy of more extended levels of parental rejection in teenagers. Side results of posttraumatic stress and shortages in friendly information dealing with were likewise related.

While rejection can harm, taking the pain of dismissal out on a person else thru intellectual mistreatment or actual violence is not regularly sound. One examine determined, as an instance, that apparent dismissal may additionally additionally upload to savagery or hostility against that amassing.

An empathetic professional can help individuals who revel in unnoticed with identifying a manner to control obvious or real dismissal and fabricate interactive abilities that could grow to be being useful to them interface all of the extra correctly with others.

Expanded Animosity: Individuals who sense socially left out are certain to view others' sports activities as being threatening and are the likely going to act in in reality detrimental techniques toward human beings they've met or interacted with or most possibly human beings whom they may have in no way interacted with.

Social Rejection

Social dismissal takes place while an individual is deliberately prohibited from a social dating or social cooperation as a form of social region. The task includes each relational rejection and heartfelt rejection. An person may be omitted on a unique premise or thru a whole amassing. Moreover, rejection may be each dynamic, through way of tormenting, prodding, or criticizing, or indifferent, through overlooking an man or woman, or giving the "quiet treatment." The revel in of being disregarded is emotional for the beneficiary, and it has a bent to be visible even as it isn't actually present.

In spite of the truth that human beings are social creatures, a few diploma of dismissal is an unavoidable piece of life. By and through, dismissal can grow to be an problem even as it's miles not on time or predictable, at the same time as the relationship is large, or whilst the character is exceptionally sensitive to dismissal. Dismissal through way of an entire amassing ought to make particularly negative outcomes, mainly even because it brings approximately pleasant detachment.

The enjoy of dismissal can prompt numerous unfriendly highbrow effects like forlornness, decreased self guarantee, animosity, and wretchedness. It can likewise activate sensations of instability and an multiplied aversion to destiny dismissal.

Acknowledgment

Rejection is sincerely hard in view of the social concept of human beings and our important should be said in gatherings. Abraham Maslow and wonderful college students have proposed that the requirement for adoration and belongingness is a primary human idea. As indicated by using manner of Maslow, everyone, even self-observers, ought to have the choice to provide and get warm temperature to be mentally sound.

Analysts reap that vital contact or social cooperation with others isn't enough to meet this want. All matters being equal, people have regions of power for a pressure to frame and preserve up with being concerned relational connections.

Individuals want every sturdy connections and thrilling collaborations with people inside the ones connections. On the off chance that each of those fixings is missing, people will start to experience desolate and troubled. Hence, dismissal is a crucial hazard. As a bear in mind of reality, most of human nerves appear to mirror problems over first-rate rejection.

Being an person from a meeting is also big for social person, it clearly is a critical part of the self-concept. Mark Leary of Wake Woodland College has proposed that the important cause for self belief is to display social own family participants and discover social dismissal. In this view, self belief is a sociometer which enacts pessimistic feelings at the same time as warning symptoms of prohibition show up.

Social intellectual examination affirms the persuasive premise of the requirement for acknowledgment. In specific, apprehension about dismissal activates adjustment to look pressure (once in a while called regulating effect), and consistence to the requests of others. Our requirement for association and social connection gives off an affect of being predominant regions of energy for especially we are below strain.

Youthful Rejection

Peer dismissal has been anticipated utilizing sociometry and distinct rating techniques. Concentrates regularly display that some kids are extensively diagnosed, getting typically high critiques, numerous children are in the center, with mild cost determinations, and minorities of children are disregarded, showing generally low fee determinations. One percentage of rejection requests that kids list peers they like and abhorrence. Rejection children get no longer many "like" assignments and hundreds of "loathe" options. Kids named not noted get not many assignments of 1 or the opposite type.

As consistent with a Clinician, it have become expressed that maximum kids who're overlooked by way of manner of their friends display at the least one of the accompanying procedures of behaving:

Low paces of prosocial conduct, as an instance alternating, sharing.

High paces of forceful or tricky way of behaving.

High paces of scatterbrained, more youthful, or incautious way of behaving.

High paces of social anxiety.

The Clinician in addition expressed that famous kids show social smart and recognize at the same time as and a manner to be part of play gatherings. Youngsters who are in risk for dismissal are effective to burst in problematically, or wait without turning into a member of via any manner. Forceful children who are athletic or have fantastic interactive capabilities are probably going to be stated with the useful resource of partners, and they'll grow to be instigators inside the provocation of tons much less gifted kids. Minority children, youngsters with incapacities, or children who have weird attributes or behavior would possibly confront extra severe risks of rejection. Contingent upon the requirements of the accomplice bunch, on occasion even minor contrasts among youngsters motive dismissal or brush aside. Youngsters who're a good deal less first-rate or essentially desire lone play are less inclined to be rejected than children who're socially restricted and supply caution signs and symptoms of frailty or uneasiness.

Peer rejection, as quickly as settled, will in trendy be ordinary over the long term, and on this manner hard for a kid to live to inform the tale. Scientists have discovered that dynamic rejection is steadier, extra hurtful, and certain to bear after a child movements to every exclusive faculty, than sincere dismiss. One justification for this is that companion bunches lay out reputational predispositions that move about as generalizations and impact resulting social communication. Hence, in any occasion, while disregarded and well-known kids show similar manner of behaving and achievements, extensively identified youngsters are treated extensively better.

Rejected kids are possibly going to have decrease self belief, and to be at more extreme gamble for incorporating troubles like despair. A few overlooked children show externalizing conduct and show hostility in place of discouragement. The examination is usually correlational, but there may be proof of same affects. This approach that youngsters with problems are wonderful to be omitted, and this rejection then turns on appreciably more outstanding issues for them. Constant friend dismissal may prompt a awful formative cycle that deteriorates with time.

Dismissed youngsters are certain to be compelled and to have fewer partners than famous youngsters; but those sports are absent all of the time. For instance, some famous children don't have pricey companions, whilst a few overlooked children do. Peer rejection is familiar to be a good deal much less harming for youngsters with a few factor like one pricey associate.

Chapter 17: Phases Of Rejection

Can we just be have a study matters objectively – coping with dismissal isn't an terrific time for absolutely everyone. It's constantly frustrating to pay interest, "you are not sufficient," after you've positioned this form of terrific deal your self in chasing after an goal, try, or project. These might not be the proper terms being verbally expressed, however they're the terms you pay attention. Take my for it, I communicate for a truth!

Here are the levels that you can experience at the same time as confronting dismissal:

Forswearing

You can't definitely be for the reason that your proposition wasn't noted. They wouldn't disregard you. Don't they recognise what your identity is? Clearly there was a few slip-up. The realtor probable intended to name some other in all likelihood client and recommended them their deal wasn't OK, considering yours certainly have become convincing.

Outrage

When you recognize there wasn't a misstep, you could start to fault the professional. You take a gander at them the same way you are taking a gander at the goods of the soil fellow at the store whilst he lets you understand they've run out of watermelons. You inquire as to whether or no longer they've got more watermelons out the lower lower back and he says no, however you understand that he realizes which you recognise he's mendacity. He's actually amassing watermelons out the again, but for motives unknown he absolutely doesn't hold which you ought to have one. For what motive didn't the professional bypass lower back to you earlier than the possibility deal have end up stated? Certainly they owed you that. Despite the truth which you apprehend the professional represents the vender and requirements to stick to their tips, they are capable of seem like the father or mom amongst you and what you want.

Melancholy

Ultimately you will likely understand the expert is an professional, and their honesty can't be offered with cupcakes or coffee. Unfortunately, you surrender to the fact you've passed up the belongings, and you can attempt and start to address at the off chance that you'll at any point see as every different home. You can't assist thinking about how you will respond at the off danger that you can't see as a domestic. Perhaps you'll want to shop for a van, start sporting an ascot and journey during the dominion settling secrets and strategies collectively along with your dog? Or but possibly you'll truely need to live on your ongoing home for eternity?

Rejection/Dismissal Responsiveness

While nobody appreciates being rejected, sure humans are extra sensitive to social rejection than others. People who are high in dismissal attention are so unfortunate and aversive to dismissal that it affects their regular sporting activities.

These human beings desire to be rejected constantly. What's extra, as they restlessly search for signs and symptoms that any individual would as a substitute now not be with them, they often act in manners that force others away. This behavior makes an excruciating cycle that can be difficult to interrupt.

People with excessive dismissal responsiveness constantly look for symptoms that they're going to be brushed off. They will more frequently than now not solution decisively to any mean that someone might as an alternative not accompany them. In mild in their feelings of trepidation and assumptions, individuals with dismissal cognizance will generally misconstrue, misshape, and overcompensate to what others say and do.

They may try to answer with hurt and outrage. Here are the elements that impact the ones overcompensations.

Increased Physiologic Action

At the point at the same time as human beings with dismissal responsiveness dread they is probably dismissed, they enjoy increased physiologic movement — more than human beings with out aversion to rejection. They furthermore live alert for additonal symptoms that they're going to be disregarded. Also, they might strive to expose survival behavior.

Confused Conduct

Touchiness to dismissal will regularly make human beings contort and misjudge the sports of others. For instance, even as companions don't solution an right now message right now, a dismissal touchy person want to anticipate, "They never over again want to be partners with me." Though any character with out dismissal responsiveness can be positive to expect the companion is truely too occupied to even maintain in thoughts answering.

Consideration Inclination

Furthermore, individuals who rank immoderate in dismissal consciousness frequently popularity nearer on dismissal or signs and symptoms and signs and symptoms and symptoms that they have been brushed off. This is known as attention inclination.

For example, assuming that any character excessive in dismissal responsiveness asked 10 people out on the town and nine acknowledged and one declined, they'll zero in the maximum on that one dismissal. They ought to try to allude to their courting endeavors as a "all out disaster" and begin to trust no man or woman likes them.

On the possibility hand, any man or woman who positions low in dismissal responsiveness ought to see similar conditions as an incredible achievement. That character may also zero in on the nine first-rate connections and provide little consideration to the handiest dismissal.

Reasons for Rejection Responsiveness

Dismissal awareness isn't brought about by one single element. All things being equal, there might be many elements at play. A few potential causes incorporate youth encounters like basic guardians and harassing, alongside natural elements and hereditary qualities. Here is a more critical gander at the variables that might prompt dismissal responsiveness.

Adolescence Encounters

Early encounters of dismissal, disregard, and manhandle may add to dismissal awareness. For instance, being presented to physical or profound dismissal by a parent might improve the probability that somebody will foster dismissal responsiveness. In any case, the dismissal doesn't necessarily should be immediate to have an effect.

Natural Weakness

Likewise figured certain individuals might have a natural weakness to dismissal responsiveness. There might be a hereditary inclination or certain character qualities that improve the probability that somebody will be delicate to dismissal. A few specialists have even connected dismissal responsiveness with low confidence, neuroticism, social nervousness, and an unreliable connection style.

Chapter 18: The Effect Of Rejection

People who experience elevated degrees of dismissal awareness experience higher levels of mental misery when they're dismissed, including close to home agony, outrage, and bitterness. While trying to manage that distress, they're likewise at a higher gamble of taking part in forcefulness, social seclusion, and self-injury.

Moreover, there are two essential variables at play in individuals with dismissal awareness: the steady should be loved and the difficulties they face in shaping significant associations with others. Here is a more critical gander at those two elements.

Consistent Reasons to be Loved

Individuals who are rejection delicate may want to be loved by everybody. Furthermore, assuming they are dismissed, they might strive to attempt to win that individual's approval once more. This response to dismissal can prompt human satisfying way of behaving as well as broad charming ways of behaving.

Heartfelt Connection Issues

Individuals who battle with dismissal responsiveness frequently decipher dismissal as evidence that they are unsatisfactory here and there. To them, dismissal is a judgment of their value and worth personally. What's more, seeing someone, this conviction framework can be terrible.

At the point when somebody is expecting dismissal, having a good sense of reassurance in relationships is hard. Regardless of whether they aren't being dismissed right now, they're continuously looking for it, anticipating that it should occur whenever, therefore, minor slips up are viewed as an all-out absence of mindful or as brutal decisions on their value personally. Eventually, the dismissal touchy individual might become upset and furious when they see an expected dismissal. Here is a more intensive glance at what dismissal responsiveness can mean for connections.

Difficulty Making Friends

A dismissal delicate individual's feeling of dread toward being dismissed makes them battle to shape new associations and to sabotage their current connections. For example, somebody who is high in dismissal responsiveness may continually blame a colleague for cheating which might add to the next individual cutting off the friendship.

Moreover, a dismissal delicate individual might become irate and threatening at whatever point a companion doesn't answer their solicitations in a convenient style. At last, that might make the companion retreat much more, which expands the feeling of dismissal.

In the meantime, others with dismissal responsiveness might keep away from all circumstances and connections where they may be dismissed. Therefore, they might feel very segregated and forlorn which basically prompts their greatest apprehensions materializing.

Chapter 19: Tips To Overcome Rejection

It's straightforward why many individuals fear and even trepidation dismissal. On the off chance that you've encountered it once, or a couple of times, you likely recall the amount it hurt and stress over it reoccurring.

In any case, dreading dismissal can keep you away from facing challenges and going after major objectives. Luckily, it's totally conceivable to manage this outlook with a touch of work. Here are a few tips to help you overcome rejection.

The vast majority need to have a place and interface with others, particularly individuals they care about. Feeling dismissed by those individuals and accepting you're not needed whether it's for a task, dating, or fellowship is certainly not a charming encounter.

The aggravation can cut pretty profound, as well. As a matter of fact, dismissal appears to activate Trusted Source the very locales in the cerebrum that actual aggravation does.

It's straightforward why many individuals fear and even trepidation dismissal. On the off chance that you've encountered it once, or a couple of times, you likely recall the amount it hurt and stress over it reoccurring.

However, dreading dismissal can keep you away from facing challenges and going after major objectives. Luckily, it's totally conceivable to manage this outlook with a touch of work. Here are a few tips to get started with:

Recall That It Happens To Everybody

Dismissal is a widespread encounter, and feeling of dread toward dismissal is extremely normal, makes sense of Brian Jones, a specialist in Seattle.

A great many people experience dismissal over things both of all shapes and sizes basically a couple of times in their lives, for example,

A companion disregarding a message about hanging out.

Being turned down for a date

Not getting a solicitation to a schoolmate's party

Approve Your Sentiments

Regardless of the wellspring of the dismissal, it actually stings. Others could see what occurred as not a problem and urge you to deal with it, yet the agony could wait, particularly on the off chance that you end up having a higher aversion to dismissal.

Rejection can likewise include other awkward feelings, like shame and clumsiness.

Nobody can let you know how you're feeling, with the exception of you. Before you can start tending to your sentiments around dismissal, recognizing them is significant. Enlightening yourself that you don't mind regarding getting injured whenever you truly do denies you the potential chance to beneficially stand up to and deal with this trepidation.

Search For The Amazing Open Door

It may not seem like an acceptable way, however rejection can give valuable open doors to self-revelation and development.

Let's assume you go after a position you truly need and have an incredible meeting, however you don't land the position. This could crush you from the start. Be that as it may, subsequent to requiring another glance at your resume, you conclude it wouldn't damage to look for any way to improve on certain abilities and figure out how to utilize another sort of programming.

Following a couple of months, you understand this new information has opened ways to more lucrative positions you beforehand weren't equipped for.

Help Yourself To Remember Your Value

Rejection can be especially terrifying when you read a lot into it. On the off chance that you've had a couple of dates with somebody who out of nowhere quits messaging back, for instance, you could concern you exhausted them or they didn't think that you are sufficiently appealing.

Yet, rejection is many times just an instance of necessities not matching up.

Ghosting is never a decent methodology, however certain individuals simply need great relational abilities or think saying, "You're overall quite charming, yet I didn't exactly feel it" could hurt you, when, truth be told, you'd truly see the value in the trustworthiness.

Developing fearlessness and self-esteem can assist you with recollecting that you're completely deserving of adoration, driving you to feel less scared of proceeding with your quest for it.

Confront Your Trepidation

Certainly, in the event that you don't put yourself out there, you won't encounter dismissal. However, you presumably will not accomplish your objectives by the same token. Going for what you maintain that gives you the opportunity should encounter achievement. You could encounter dismissal however at that point once more, you could not.

Keep Things In Context

On the off chance that you're more delicate to dismissal and invest a ton of energy stressing over it, you could envision a ton of most pessimistic scenario situations.

Let's assume you didn't get into your alumni program of decision. You could begin stressing that every one of the projects you applied to will dismiss you and you'll need to attempt in the future one year from now.

However at that point you start to stress that you'll be dismissed one year from now which will make it difficult to land the position you need and advance your vocation, which will make it incomprehensible for you to at any point turn out to be monetarily sufficiently stable to accomplish your fantasy of homeownership and a family, etc.

Reject Negative Self-Talk

It's not difficult to fall into an example of self-analysis in the wake of encountering rejection. You could make statements like, "I realized I'd wreck that," "I didn't plan enough," "I blabbered," or "I'm so exhausting."

In any case, this simply supports your conviction that the dismissal was your shortcoming when it might have had nothing to do with you by any means. In the event that you are accepted, somebody will rejection you since you're not sufficient, this dread can push ahead with you and become an unavoidable outcome.

Positive reasoning doesn't necessarily in all cases make circumstances turn out a specific way, however it can assist with working on your point of view. At the point when you empower and uphold yourself, you're bound to have confidence in your own capability to accomplish your objectives.